Lost Cornwall

Lost Cornwall

REDISCOVERED THROUGH HISTORIC PHOTOGRAPHS
FROM THE REG WATKISS ARCHIVE

COMPILED AND WRITTEN BY
REG WATKISS

HALSGROVE

First published in Great Britain in 2004
Reprinted 2005, 2007

British Library Cataloguing-in-Publication Data
A CIP record for this title is available from the British Library

ISBN 978 1 84114 365 1

HALSGROVE

Halsgrove House
Ryelands Industrial Estate
Bagley Road, Wellington
Somerset TA21 9PZ
Tel: 01823 653777
Fax: 01823 216796
email: sales@halsgrove.com
website: www.halsgrove.com

Printed and bound in Great Britain by
CPI Antony Rowe Ltd., Chippenham, Wiltshire

CONTENTS

ACKNOWLEDGEMENTS

A list of the identified photographers included in this work is given here, and throughout the supporting text certain of these are referred to again in more detail. With the exception of Henry Fox Talbot, placed first because of his importance as a founder of photography, the others are given in alphabetical order: J.C. Burrow ARPS of Camborne; Charles Roberts Chapple of St Levan; Francis Frith; Gibson & Sons of Penzance and the Scilly Isles; Govier of St Buryan; John W.C. Gutch of Bristol; W.M. Harrison of Falmouth; A.W. Hughes; William Jenkyn (possibly!); Arthur Janes of Enterprise Studio Bodmin; Charles Lobb of Wadebridge; Vaugh T. Paul of Penzance; Robert Preston of Penzance; J.F. McClary of Drift, Penzance; Richards Bros of Penzance; the Thorn family of photographers, Bude; William Thomas of Ballowal, St Just-in-Penwith; and Edwin Trembath of St Just-in-Penwith.

There are many photographs which cannot positively be ascribed. Some are obviously the work of professionals but others are by gifted amateurs and still others, such as one of the final images in the book of the postman, Mr Osborne, are the result of an inspired, or well timed, snapshot.

Over the years that I have been collecting I have been helped by many people with the loan of prints, gifts of prints and plates, and support interest. It would be difficult to list all of these people but the extra special contribution of some must, I feel, be mentioned. Clive Carter has been of particular help in documenting the shipwrecks and confirming some of the industrial details generally. Clive is almost a one-man walking encyclopaedia of facts and related stories. The careful research given in Professor Charles Thomas's book *Views and Likenesses* has been most useful, leading to the St Just, John Gutch discovery. Recent offers, made by Brian Pannell of Penzance, to make available examples of some of his stereo prints, and also by Howard Whitt of Mousehole, who loaned original stereo plates, assisted in that section. Important contributions were made in the past by George Burrow, grandson of J.C. Burrow ARPS, who loaned me a copy of *'Mongst Mines and Miners* with its original photographic illustrations, plus other things by his grandfather. Dr Godfrey Symonds' contribution, many years ago, was a great boost to my collection and of course, Alathea Garstin was really responsible, during one chance afternoon, for getting me going in the first place.

Pat Pilkington's contribution from her excellent collection of Newlyn prints has to be mentioned, with many thanks again, as do the two rare and interesting Le Grice family group portraits of the 1850s, supplied also some years ago, separately, by Jeremy Le Grice and Cordelia Dobson. John Smith, my colleague of some years, I thank for his part in promoting this opportunity by first bringing my collection to the attention of Halsgrove.

Among others recently who have given help and shown interest are Michael Eddy, whose knowledge of the retail life of Penzance over the century is an excellent key to dating street scenes. Peter London of Hampshire, author of *Aviation in Cornwall*, has been enthusiastic in his efforts to supply data and as such, is a very reliable source. Thanks also to Alan Austin for allowing me to access some of the Harrison prints, and Rubina Craze for her contribution and assistance with details regarding Zennor. To all those who have loaned or contributed over the years, I'd like to offer my general thanks.

I have been offered ready assistance from the following people and institutions, when requested: Elaine George, Town Clerk of St Just-in-Penwith; Angela Broome, Librarian of the Courtney library in the Royal Institution of Cornwall and Robert Cooke their Photographic Curator; Alison Lloyd, Curator of the Penlee House Gallery and Museum, Penzance; the staff of the Penzance Morrab Gardens private library and the staff of the Penzance County Library.

Finally, I'd like to thank the directors of Halsgrove for the opportunity to publish this collection and Simon Butler in particular, for the enthusiasm he has shown, and for the number of journeys he has made down to West Cornwall to view progress and add advice and encouragement.

INTRODUCTION

It was at the beginning of the 1960s that I first met and became friends with the painter Alathea Garstin, daughter of Norman Garstin, also a painter who is remembered, among other things, as being one of the co-founders of the Newly School of artists established in the late nineteenth century. One afternoon in Alathea's studio we were discussing the possible influences photography had made on the work of these artists, a topic prompted by me, as the use painters made of the photographic image had been an interest of mine since my early days as an art student. The thesis produced for my NDD was 'The influences of photography on art', and my studies as a painter had been carried on in tandem with a part-time photographic course. As the conversation continued Alathea fetched from a cupboard a ribbon-tied folder, which she opened carefully to reveal a small collection of whole-plate photographic prints of West Cornwall. They were mostly from the late-Victorian period and Edwardian. Certainly, in the examples of these Alathea presented, one couldn't ignore the similarities between them and certain of the Newlyn School artists' compositions, and general treatment of the subject. Alathea went on to explain that some of the prints had belonged to her father, whilst others had been purchased by her as a young woman directly from the photographers' establishments in Penzance: Gibson & Sons on The Terrace, Robert Preston's studio further up Market Jew Street by the Market House, Richards Bros in Queen Street and Vaughan T. Paul's Morrab Road studio.

The importance for me of this chance display was that these photographs represented my first introduction to the original prints of these West Penwith photographers, which I at once felt were remarkable in many ways. I still remember clearly being bowled over by the beauty of certain images: 'Fish Jousters on Newly Beach' of 1885 was one, and 'Old School Slip', also of 1885, was another, both the work of the Gibsons. What was so impressive also, viewing all the examples Alathea produced, was the clarity of the images. The superb control of available light which brought to mind, in some examples, the pictures of the Impressionist painters, and also the sensitive treatment of the content their obvious technical skill had allowed them to achieve. Previously, for my student thesis, I had become aware of certain names in contemporary British photographic histories, Sutcliffe, Peach Robinson, Francis Frith etc., as landscape photographers, and I could not understand why the names of at least some of these Cornish photographers had not so far featured in a national representative history of photography.

I realised however, beyond our immediate conversation that afternoon, I had discovered what was to become a lasting enthusiasm, and one that although concerned with the pursuit of images from the past, would in fact open up Cornwall to me in a totally new and exciting way. Alathea was very pleased to let me make copies, which formed the beginnings of my collection, and I set about hunting out further examples in all manner of locations. Today the collection fills a number of cabinets with copy negatives, original prints, plates and supporting items.

There soon evolves a need to do something more with a collection of almost anything, than just hiding it away. In this case, being visual, it needed exhibiting or displaying in some way.

That's how several books I did in the mid 1970s came about, as I was offered publication support. Those books were quite well received and I was able in them to convey my early enthusiasm and some discoveries so that others could enjoy them too. I must admit however, that by the completion of the last of these I was partly convinced that I had probably exhausted most of the sources for acquiring new images, at least from the early years of photography in the area. Other specialist books had of course also been published on a variety of themes: wrecks, ancient history, mining etc. How wrong I was in this assumption. Following publication, the books themselves stimulated people to approach me to discuss their content further, telling me of the photographic treasures they had stuffed in kitchen cupboards or fish lofts, bicycle sheds, and, as usual, the attic. Single prints and whole albums suddenly showed up. The tranquil and beautiful 'Port Navas' by Harrison of Falmouth was in one of these album collections. Dusty bundles of original plates revealed delightful, untold stories, like the half plates of the old knife grinder and little girl, and the old man with donkey on the north coast. Chance meetings with owners of rare archive images brought to light the Newlyn seaplane port, locked in tattered vest-pocket Kodak negatives of 1917.

Possibly my most exciting find of the last decade is the John Wheely Gough Gutch print of 'the Market Place, St Just, and church',1858, as he titled it. As rare as his name, when found this was just holding its own (only just!). Along with the active woodworm in the oak frame and a menagerie of dead moths and forgotten spiders trapped between the splintered backing board, it was still with its original Penzance framer's label.

These then are references to just some of the high points that have added renewed interest and fun to my collecting since the mid seventies, boosting the collection into the thousands.

The invitation by Simon Butler of Halsgrove to make this selection for publication was an offer I was very pleased to accept. It was made at so right a time for me, since an investigation of files and folders, envelopes and box contents I had consigned to dark corners over the past two decades was now desperately overdue. During the effort of sorting through things I have come across images I'd almost forgotten I ever had, and made contact once again with others I've been searching for in all the wrong places for several years.

Included here are the restoration results of many cracked and discoloured plates and prints. Enhancing of certain images has only been carried out by traditional photographic techniques, where necessary. The John Gutch photograph of St Just, for instance, would not have been reasonably viewable if printed as found, but by contrast manipulation in both the copy negative I made and in the enlargement, the atmosphere and content of the picture has been, as near as possible, truthfully conveyed. No brush line additions, or electronic or laser enhancing of images has taken place. It's not that these very modern techniques aren't useful, it's just they are not, I feel, appropriate for this archive presentation.

In all but a few cases the whole of the print as the photographer originally presented it has been reproduced here. One or two of the cracked plates have a part of the image missing. Marazion station in the snow is one of these; the right hand has lost about an inch. The stereo pairs have all been given an, approximately, three-inch base, that means division between a selected infinity point. Stereo afficionados will be critical of this, saying it should be 68mm, but my experience is that for free viewing, as I'm suggesting readers attempt in this section, a three-inch slightly larger scale base is easier overall for the purpose, especially if people are shortsighted. Reading glasses should be kept on for free viewing.

The finding of two-hundred-and-fifty plus prints, as discussed with Simon Butler, has not been a difficult one from the many I have, though I've left out some, with reluctance. Some difficulty was, however, encountered in deciding on a structure for their presentation. In the end I have settled on a fairly loose grouping by region which offers the freedom to browse at random while reflecting on my years of collecting that I can claim has been catholic in choice. The photographic impact, whatever the subject, has largely taken precedence in this but, that said, I've also kept in mind the overall rarity of the documentation and historic value of a photograph.

The dominance of photographs from the west and south-west of the county is due, in most part, to my residence for over forty years in West Penwith, presenting the greater chance of acquiring examples of this region. However, it is fair also to say that the west of the county has been the base of more photographers of note, particularly in the earlier part of the twentieth century and the nineteenth century from the 1850s onwards. This has made the availability of examples of work that much easier to come by, for all the obvious reasons. I do have a fairly large number of examples of the Thorn family's work of Bude in North Cornwall, but they are mostly documenting the continual misfortune of the ships, large and small, which met their end on that treacherous coastline, and this is not a book only about shipwrecks. This theme has been well covered in Clive Carter's book *Cornish Shipwrecks – The North Coast*. Nevertheless, some good examples of their work are included.

The photographs are supported by captions of varying length. I make no claims to being an historian, though a wealth of interesting facts and stories have followed in the wake of the photographic acquisitions over the years. However, where specific dates and data generally had been given, every attempt has been made to ensure it is correct, and I have gone to a number of specialist sources, wherever necessary, so that the reader can, with some confidence, use for reference the information given. One must be alert however, in weighing up information supplied, especially if there's a good yarn surrounding an historical event!

I have already defined the reasons providing the impetus behind this publication. It will make the many hours I spent in the photographic darkroom over some months seem that much more worthwhile once the images are positively arranged and put together. I hope fun and entertainment will be very much a part of the book's appeal. If it further provokes comment and conversation, inspires others to collect, or extracts from obscurity further photographic finds, as has been my experience before, that will be a bonus.

'Enough!' I hear someone cry out. 'Let the photographs speak for themselves.'

It's probably a plea for peace in our time from my daughter Louise in her little cottage down Chapel Street, coping to the last with my appalling handwriting and scratchy alterations as she nears the end of typing all this. So let it be!

It's always been true that one good picture is worth a thousand words.

Reg Watkiss
Penzance 2004

Carclew House, 1841

I am starting this book with a print dating from the very beginnings of photography. It was in September of 1840 that William Henry Fox Talbot discovered the negative positive process using sensitised paper, calling the result calotypes, later also referred to as talbotypes. It is reliably documented that Fox Talbot visited Carclew House, near Truro, in 1841, the home of his uncle by marriage, Sir Charles Lemon FRS, and whilst there made exposures. Another guest of Sir Charles, present at the same time, John Sterling, also refers to Talbot's 'photogenic' activities in a letter to his wife. In 1844 Talbot set up a calotype printing establishment in Reading, the first in the world, and between 1844 and 1847, when he closed it, thousands of calotypes were made there from earlier and current negatives, for sale to stationers and publishers. I was fortunate to be given this rare copy negative by a photographer friend some thirty years ago, who had been involved in documenting a number of Talbot's early calotypes in London. The two women on the balcony are nieces of Sir Charles, the one on the right identified by reference to another print as Louisa Amy Dyke, and it would appear the man with the walking stick is Sir Charles himself. Enlarging from the quite small original has in this instance I feel emphasised the powerful composition Talbot has achieved of this once grand house. The soft early Victorian sunlight that bathes the stonework and figures is further amplified by the quality the paper negative process imparts to the print. The ghost of a house, that was destroyed by fire in 1934, rises from the page to engage our thoughts and senses.

EARLY PHOTOGRAPHS

Market Place, St Just, 1858
From an original albumen print

At precisely 3.40pm, as we can see by the St Just-in-Penwith church clock, during a Saturday market of August 1858, John Gutch exposed the wet plate in his wooden and brass camera to record this summer afternoon scene. He was a Bristol-based photographer and during that month was to photograph many locations in West Cornwall. The mixed group of gentlemen, crinolined ladies, townspeople and traders seen here, almost one hundred and fifty years later, viewed by the light of a day, now so distant, has a fascination for me that has lasted throughout my forty years of collecting photographic images. There is a particular hazy magic in this and quite often other very early albumen and talbotype prints. Professor Charles Thomas in his publication for the Royal Institution of Cornwall, *Views and Likenesses* (1988), gives reliable details of Gutch, as he does of a number of other early photographers in the county. He explains how E. Rowe of Penzance, a bookseller, and Mr Weston of Bristol, published one hundred John Wheeley Gough Gutch prints, giving all titles, available in 8.5 x 6.5in albumen prints. Still holding plenty of detail, I did have to carefully enhance the contrast when enlarging my copy negative in order to bring the image to a level that made it generally viewable. It was fully titled in a fine Victorian handwriting on the grime-covered board. Sold as St Just Market Place and Church 1858, we now know this location as St Just Square, and by the end of the nineteenth century, market day was officially on a Thursday. The Kings Arms in the background is still so named today. How nice to think that some things don't change.

Market Jew Street, c.1855

Since I presented this photograph of Penzance in my first book, thirty years ago, I have made further attempts to attribute it to a photographer and confirm the date. I now feel that the date is a little later than I gave then, of 1851, though that had been based on detailed observation of the scene. It has been suggested that William Jenkyn, who was a photographer in the town from 1853 onwards, could be the author of it. On finding the firmly identifiable photograph of St Just by John Gutch (previous page) and by comparing the image quality, I have considered the fact that there are similarities in the direction of ceremony and arrangement of the people, thus he might also have made this print in that August of 1858. For certain The Star portico, on the left of this picture, was knocked down in 1860. Whatever, it is a splendid glimpse of a Victorian street, and using the slow wet-plate process it would have presented plenty of problems for the photographer.

Penzance Station, 1868

The earliest photograph of the station in my collection. I made this copy after much effort from a faded image on a *carte-de-visit* style card some twenty years ago. It has since been published several times from my prints without a by-your-leave and also wrongly dated! It is in fact a photograph of 1868 and was taken two years after Brunel's broad gauge came to Penzance. The locomotive, loaned from the South Devon Railway, was a broad gauge 440 saddle tank, the *Antelope*. She was withdrawn from service in 1884. Several details are worthy of note. The locomotive turntable in the foreground, the fish boxes and baskets, giving a clue to the enhanced trade the railways had brought to the local industry, and on the centre top the clear mound of ancient Lescudjack Castle.

Penzance, 1884

The opening ceremony of the Penzance floating dock in November 1884. Nearest to the quay is *Queen of the Bay* owned and used by the West Cornwall Steamship Company on the Penzance-to-Scilly service.

Penzance Harbour, c.1869

A tranquil Penzance harbour in 1869 or just before. I would like to attribute it to Robert Preston since it has all the quality and style of his best work, but the print isn't identified. Preston's prints are usually stamped or printed on the back 'Robert.H.Preston photographer to the Prince and Princess of Wales'. He was the official photographer when the Royal pair came to visit Botallack Mine in 1865.

Wood Street, Penzance, c.1860

A thatched shop in Penzance at the junction of Wood Street with Market Jew Street. This was one of quite a number of thatched buildings to be found in the town around the 1860s when this photograph was made. What a pity we cannot see the notices clearly on this side of Langley's Stores. The whole building was burnt down in 1889, including that of the Ellis Dairy next door up.

The Green Market, Penzance, 1860

A fine early example of the work of the photographer Robert Preston. The Three Tuns Hotel was run by George Hemmings up to 1859, when he died, and then the family continued in the business until 1864. The old Market Cross is clearly seen at this the start of Causewayhead. In the original print the name of Hemmings can just be made out over the main door of the hotel.

Captain Tonkin

In the 1850s glass collodion negatives were often mounted in front of a framed black background to give a positive effect. It was an inexpensive method of making a gift or commemorative portrait. Sometimes these were quite elaborately presented in a hinged-box frame. They were known as collodion positives in England and ambrotypes in America, the latter name now universally adopted.

This portrait is from an ambrotype shown to me thirty years ago by the then very old Cordelia Dobson of Newlyn whose aged grandmother had given it to her. Cordelia recounted the tragic story of Captain Tonkin of Newlyn Manor, the subject of the photograph, who came to a sad end after his vessel was boarded in the China Seas by pirates and he was made to walk the plank!

The family of Charles Valentine Le Grice of Trereiffe, Penzance

These two group portrait studies were taken on the same day, for although there are certain marked differences in them, though obvious compositional similarity, the real clue that promotes this fact is the identical nature of the vegetation seen on the left of both pictures. They were, I know, taken with two different cameras as I used original plates to make the prints presented here. In any case, image and detail sharpness is not the same. It seems likely that more than one photographer was present, perhaps an arranged party of students from the Regent House School of Art, founded in 1853 under its Head H.M. Geoffroi, who in its first year, we are told, presented 'a fine collection of photographs', and who no doubt went on in the following years to do the same. The Penzance Grammar School also had a master at that time promoting photography. Charles Valentine Le Grice was much connected with the school in his lifetime.

An interesting, if minor, fact relating to one of the plates shown to me by the near-ninety-year-old Cordelia Dobson of Newlyn in the 1970s, is one that her ninety-eight-year-old grandmother recounted to her when Cordelia was a small girl: 'I saw that boy, Charles Valentine Le Grice first when he came down to tutor, sitting in an apple tree at Trereiffe orchard. He was throwing apples at me.' That story, handed down by word of mouth, happened approximately two hundred years ago!

The Longships Lighthouse, 1860s

This photograph, by Nicholas Blake Lobb, is of the first Longships lighthouse. Standing on Carn Bras Rock, it was a three-storey building having a base just 40 feet above sea level. It was 78 feet high to the fixed octagonal lantern. Begun in 1791 its light was often obscured in very heavy seas so a replacement was built. A new light operated from the 114-foot tower we see today, for the first time in December 1873.

Mining in the 1850s

This view of mine workings in West Cornwall dates from the 1850s. The whole-plate albumen original I copied it from was owned by a family living in St Just, near to Botallack, which is where I think this is. In style and technique it could be attributed to John Gutch. Rowe the bookseller and publisher whose advert is illustrated in Professor Charles Thomas' book *Views and Likenesses*, lists among prints for sale in 1858, 'Group of Miners, Botallack Mine'. It presents a fine picture of a horse-whim used for winding up the ore placed in the kibble, seen lying in the foreground. The horse was harnessed to the vertical shaft seen attached to the cross-beam and walked around. The man with the stove-pipe hat could be the mine captain.

The *Gannet*, Morvah Cliffs, 1871

In 1851 the collodion negative was introduced by Frederick Scott Archer. This became known as the wet-plate process, since glass plates, once sensitised, had to be exposed and developed immediately, before the collodion coating dried. The greatly improved detail achieved by this process, and the marked shortening of exposure times, led to it replacing the calotype process. Wet-plate photography did present problems with outside subjects, landscape, documentary etc., since a fair amount of processing equipment had to be carried along with the camera for immediate application. Certainly, a shipwreck off a Cornish cliff was not the easiest of subjects. It is notable that until about the 1880s, just after the introduction of faster dry-plates in 1878, photographs of vessels in distress are limited. This print was not acknowledged, but could be by Trembath of nearby St Just-in-Penwith. It shows *The Gannet*, a 560-ton iron steam sailing packet, having run ashore in fog under Morvah cliff on 28 May 1871. She was carrying a general cargo from Liverpool to Antwerp.

Bodmin Jail, 1880s

Bodmin Jail was built during the 1780s by Napoleonic prisoners of war. The first hanging there is given as 1785, though the finishing date for the building is given as 7 March 1788. Awe is very much the effect the first sight of Bodmin Jail has on most people even today. Now mostly a ruin, apart from the main entrance building which has become a tavern with adjoining museum, how much more sinister and terrible would a prisoner have viewed his fate on approach to it in the 1870s, when this photograph was taken. Published by Arthur James of Enterprise Studio, Honey Street and Turf Street, Bodmin, he obviously wished to gain from the sale of this card to tourists.

William Calcraft was the established and respected expert hangman for Cornwall at the time. Is that him (inset) on the card, waiting with his bag of instruments and tools, before entering the main jail gates. The Enterprise Studio would certainly have considered his presence on the card as a sure selling feature. In its one hundred and fifty years of existence 55 prisoners were executed here, all by hanging, and 51 of those hangings were public.

Later, when a new wing was to be added, the erection of an execution drop on the north side of the jail was considered, but this idea was abandoned by the authorities as it was felt that fewer members of the public would be able to view executions! William Calcraft and other executioners were paid £10 a hanging. He was also engaged to supervise floggings. The last man to be executed at the jail was from St Erth. Convicted in 1909 for a crime of passion, he is said to have given himself up to the local policeman who was on his bicycle at St Erth Station.

The jail closed in 1927. A depressing list of early hangings tells of young men being hanged for such trivial offences as stealing three sheep, stealing a gold ring, and stealing a print.

PENZANCE AND NEWLYN

The Harbour, Penzance, 1870s

The Abbey Slip is extreme right, with Coulson's Granary and a coastal schooner immediately below St Mary's Church. On the left is Mathews' shipbuilders, together with their steam saw mills. Prior to the building of the floating dock in 1879, and its completion in 1884, vessels would have come right up to these buildings awaiting or discharging cargoes, laying up between tides.

Plymouth Sailing Trawler, early 1870s

This finely-composed print by the Gibsons shows how busy Penzance harbour was even before the completion of the floating dock in 1884. Plymouth fishing boats (designated PH) used Penzance and Newlyn frequently during the fishing season. The tight groups of vessels laid up in the background are mostly local schooners and barques. The Albert Pier is on the right.

Fishing Boats, Penzance

Penzance looking towards the Abbey Slip, Coulson's Granary and St Marys' Church. Piles just visible to the left of the mast (left foreground) are for the start of the floating dock, so that dates this photograph to 1879. Along with St Mary's Church and Coulson's Granary, the old Penzance Bath House and a ships' chandler, can be seen at the water's edge.

Penzance Dock, 1909

This is the *Leon Bureau,* with the salvage ship *Green Castle* alongside her. On 1 June 1909 she hit the Crim rocks off the Scilly Isles, making a sizeable hole in her hull. After making her way with difficulty to Mount's Bay she was towed into Penzance dock.

Market Jew Street, 1870s

Looking south-west up Market Jew Street in Penzance. This has been one of the most photographed streets in Cornwall over the century and a half since photography began. This early view is a great favourite of mine, taken by the Gibsons early in the morning, as the shadows indicate. There is blurring of some figures as a result of the long exposure, and this time of day was obviously chosen to avoid having to contend with too much movement. This leads to the conclusion that the photograph was almost certainly

taken before the faster dry plates of 1878 were generally available and adopted by most photographers. I have formerly dated it to the late 1870s, early 1880s, but feel fairly convinced that the first of these is right. The Humphry Davy commemorative statue in front of the Market House was erected in 1872.

Market Jew Street, 1880s

Looking down Market Jew Street, Penzance in the 1880s. On the left of the picture, at Oppenheims, is the birthplace of the Cornish inventor Humphry Davy, best known for his invention of the miners' safety lamp. Among his other achievements is the first published account of a photographic process. This appeared in the journal of the Royal Institution for June 1802 as 'an account of a method of copying paintings upon glass and of making profiles by the agency of light upon nitrates of silver, invented by T. Wedgewood with observations by H. Davy'. In Wedgewood's attempt to fix his 'sun pictures', as he called them, Davy had advised him from 1791 onwards. Today taxis still wait where landaus and other horse-drawn vehicles once plied their trade.

Penzance Promenade

Photographed in the later part of King Edward VII's reign, the scene is the junction on the promenade with the bottom of Alexandra Road. The splendid centrepiece, topped with its gas lamp, commemorates the opening of Alexandra Road by Alexandra, Princess of Wales, Duchess of Cornwall, on 24 July 1865. This feature was moved at some later date to a location near the rugby club, where it now stands, almost unnoticed and minus the lamp. On this same day in 1865, the Princess also made a visit to St Just-in-Penwith and was shown around the Crowns Mine, Botallack.

21

The Royal Baths, Boarding and Lodging House, c.1880

Also advertised as Mr Norton's Royal Promenade Spa Baths, these were located midway between the Queens Hotel and Alexandra Road, on the main Penzance promenade. The whole complex was demolished in 1883 but not before the photographers, Gibsons, had used an end part of it, as can be seen, for their first Penzance print shop and studio from the middle of the 1870s. This photograph, I would say, made using the new dry plates available from 1878 onwards, can then be dated as between 1878–83. The definition that could be achieved using the fine-grain whole-plate negative was quite remarkable in the hands of a good professional photographer.

Whilst making this print from my copy negative of an original, I decided to experiment a little and racked up my enlarger to print up the small section that shows the old Wherry Town coastguard house and station and attached lifeboat house. I've included it here as you can even see the cannon used to summon the lifeboat crew in an emergency. This can be picked out just left under the station flagpole. The *Richard Lewis* lifeboat was in service at this time, her years being 1865–84. There is an earlier view of the coastguard and lifeboat station dated to the 1860s, by Robert Preston, but the technical aids then available in no way allowed him to approach the quality of this image.

Sails in Mount's Bay, c.1900

A busy scene in Mount's Bay at the end of the nineteenth century, with a brigantine making its way through the Newlyn fishing fleet bound for Penzance harbour.

The Green Market, Penzance

The photographer, Gibson, had to be standing in the middle of the road to get this view of the Green Market, or was there in those days some other road traffic arrangement? The two cars are stationed with no one at the wheel. Was it, I have wondered since I purchased the plate over twenty-five years ago, taken for advertising purposes? Perhaps it was commissioned by Timothy Whites, who opened on 16 May 1915 (Michael Eddy, an authority on trading over the century in Penzance, is my source for this). It was published elsewhere some years ago using a print I had made but without reference to me, and with incorrect datings.

The *Jeune Hortense*
ashore in Mount's Bay, 17 May 1888

This is a well-known and well-published photograph made by the Gibsons but I'm including it because, for me, no representative collection of archive photography can properly claim to be so without it. In spite of various aficionados declaring that photography is not art, I think differently, and consider this to be one of the masterpieces of nineteenth-century reportage photography. The photographer has, under what would have been quite extreme and urgent physical and technical conditions, realised just when to open the shutter to capture the drama of the occasion at its height, as the lifeboat, *Dora*, returns with the crew of the *Hortense*.

One could almost believe that the placement of the horseman and the boy has been arranged. They seem so brilliantly positioned, taking the eye up to the stormy sky, then over and round to St Michael's Mount and back again to the silhouetted crowd. But it is not contrived, nor did the photographer have any control over the weather. He couldn't manipulate the length of exposure much either but, like Cartier Bresson, the great twentieth-century master photographer, he has realised an inspired moment.

This would not have been achieved by luck but by the accumulated knowledge of his craft, how the image would be committed to the whole plate in the camera, the moment frozen by light. At this time the French Impressionists were putting their manifesto into practice in another medium, paint. Musicians and poets were conveying the ideas that light, which illuminated the instant moment, was the purveyor of reality; the achievement of art being to hold and convey the experience to others. Of course this photograph is a work of art. It is a photograph which has inspired photographers since, and who have projected through their medium their personal vision of things in such a way as to make it of value to others.

It is not known which of the two Gibson brothers in the Penzance firm actually took the photograph. Alexander and Herbert probably worked together on many assignments. I have three shots of the event. The first shows the ship some way off along the beach, obviously a snatched exposure as they arrived quickly at the scene with the lifeboat in service. Then this picture was made. The third is of the lifeboat on its carriage. I have heard of a fourth but I have not been able to locate a copy. The others do not match the superb quality of this image but they do, for a variety of reasons, give a clue to difficult weather conditions hampering the photographer's efforts. Camera shake, water on lenses and plates, viewing the set up quickly on the camera's back screen under a black cloth with a huge wind blowing, would have tested their skills to the full. The first hurried shot gives evidence of the photographer not being fully adjusted to the situation prior to achieving this fine image a short time later.

I have seen this scene captioned several times in publications, with the statement that the lifeboat *Richard Lewis* was in attendance. This cannot be so, the *Richard Lewis* was taken out of service in 1884 and from

1884–95 RNLI records show that the 3-ton *Dora*, official number 49, was on station at Penzance and was the boat launched to the rescue of the *Hortense* in 1888. Thomas Carbis, however, was the coxswain for many years on both lifeboats, in the period 1873–91, and this could have led to some confusion in the records. The *Jeune Hortense* had been on passage from Brest to Fowey when driven ashore on Eastern Green, Penzance, by the south-westerly gale.

Penzance Station, c.1870

Captioned in several publications as 'a rare view of Penzance station', it is rapidly becoming less rare, being used in several books on the history of the Great Western Railway. I used it in my first book in 1975 but, all things considered, it is not a print that can properly be left out of a collection like this as it is both an excellent photograph of the station, and of the gateway to Penzance. It does as well offer a unique glimpse of the mixed gauge running that operated on the Great Western Railway in Cornwall and Devon from November 1866, until 21 May 1892, passenger services beginning over it from 1 March 1867. The dual gauge system seen in the photograph was quite often used by mixed-gauge rolling stock, with the goods train using an adaptor wagon of special construction to act as a separator.

In 1892, in just two days on 20 and 21 May, the seven-foot GWR gauge was lifted throughout Cornwall and into Devon as far as Exeter, leaving only the standard 4ft 8in gauge now used. One wonders if such a feat could be accomplished by today's railway companies.

Marazion Station

A visit of Edward, Prince of Wales, or Edward VII, King of England. The date of the photograph is unknown but by looking at the fashions, it is probable that this is the 1907 visit of King Edward VII. He would of course have been entertained by Lord and Lady St Levan on St Michael's Mount, close by the station. It doesn't look a very good day for his visit.

Come to Sunny Cornwall!

Two further views of Penzance station, both with a rainy-day look. The first, taken approximately thirty years or so after the photograph on the facing page, appeals very much to me for the sheer impact of this image, captured by the photographers Richards Bros, in obviously heavy weather conditions. That below, also by Richards Bros, was taken as the train makes for the station shelter with a south-easterly gale battering into it. With the construction of the new sea wall in 1937 and general widening of the station area this scene, with its visual drama, became more infrequent.

Marazion, 1947

This Christmas-card scene of Marazion station in the snow of 1947 (as far as can be established), is also by Richards Bros. The station is no longer standing, apart from one dilapidated building!

Newlyn Quarry Locomotive, Newlyn

The Great Western Railway couldn't claim the record of being the most south-westerly in England. That accolade went to the Penlee Quarry two-foot narrow gauge railway at Newlyn. Approximately one mile long, it ran from the end of the South Pier (Stone Boat Pier as it came to be called) to works on the cliff road to Mousehole.

Penlee Quarry, 1930s

This is Penlee Quarry's top locomotive driver, 'Janner', about whom there are many stories, most of which are probably untrue. The one I like best is that when he turned his bowler hat around the locomotive went the other way! The locomotive was built in Berlin in 1901. For those narrow-gauge enthusiasts who might wish to know, I myself photographed her from all angles in the 1960s, as she stood, a sad reminder of her former days, on a concrete plinth where the quarry had retired her. The south-easterly gales and salt water were beginning to tell on her fabric but my shots would supply a modeller with all the necessary information. She was eventually taken away by a preservation society.

Penlee Quarry

Penlee Quarry locomotive; this time a splendid, front on, boiler view, but who's that driving Janner's steam engine?

28

Stone Boat Pier, Newlyn

A stone boat waiting to be loaded with fine chippings on the South Pier, often referred to as Stone Boat Pier. A very exciting composition is achieved by the texture and linear patterns of the varying industrial elements, while the workers' portraits add to the overall animation and interest of the scene.

The *Janet Hoyle*, c.1915

The *Janet Hoyle* was on service in Penzance from 1912 until 1917, having formerly been stationed at Ayr in Scotland. Here she is seen off Penzance lighthouse pier.

Penzance Promenade,
latter part of the 1870s

The Royal Promenade Baths can be seen just to the left of the Queens Hotel. As stated elsewhere, these were demolished in 1883. The sand over which the pilchard nets are laid only disappeared from the foreshore after the North Pier was completed in 1894. Those with a detailed knowledge of the locality have put forward the theory that the pier altered the tidal flow in such a way that sand was swept round and out to sea. Others have suggested that the removal of wooden groynes that once were set at intervals along the length of the beach was responsible.

Penzance Promenade, c.1910

This charming scene was something of a set-up by the photographers working for the Frith postcard company. The three women on the left, resplendent in identical dresses and hats, appear walking up and down the promenade in other postcards, obviously on the same sunny day, either in front of the Queens Hotel, as here, or further along with more of the sea in the background.

Elizabeth and Blanche Lifeboat, c.1910

The lifeboat *Elizabeth and Blanche* was moved from Penzance to Newlyn in 1908 to overcome problems launching her in Penzance. She was located here below the cliff road on the area of harbour foreshore between the South Pier and the old harbour. During the five years, until 1913, that she was stationed in Newlyn, Alfred Vingoe was coxswain, and from 1910–13, T.E. Vingoe. Another view of her can be seen in the stereo pairs section of this collection. It's one of the best views I've seen, giving a clear, well composed depiction of a sailing lifeboat.

Newlyn Fishing Fleet, c.1900

The Newlyn fishing fleet leaving harbour on the evening tide for the pilchard fishing in Mount's Bay. Enormous shoals of these fish supported the Cornish industry in the late-nineteenth and early-twentieth centuries. In 1960 I went out one night for a trip from Newlyn on a pilchard driver. What amazed me was the way you could so strongly smell the fish once we arrived over them and shot the nets. Mixed with the reek of diesel from the boat's engine, various other smells, and the heat down below from a small coal fire, it's an experience I will not forget. I declined the tea and ham sandwiches which I was offered and went back up on deck quite quickly!

Newlyn, 1871

There is something quite extraordinary about the dynamic patterns and almost abstract quality captured by the photographer, who I think was Robert Preston, in his selected viewpoint for this picture of Newlyn foreshore. It is taken from a location which now approximates to various harbour offices. The content is also illuminating, showing as it does the many hundreds of baskets, washing skips and barrels necessary to support the fishing industry of the town. Now all the basket-makers have gone, the last being Clarence Wallis, who retired some years ago. In 1888 the river was diverted so that work could begin on the short arm of the North Pier.

Newlyn, c.1900

Washing barking pans and baskets in Newlyn river. More detailed reference to the practice of barking nets is given in relation to the Mousehole print showing nets hung out to dry (page 45).

Newlyn Coombe, 1870s

Looking upriver and Newlyn Coombe from the old bridge area in the 1870s. The white thatched cottage seen on the right was the house in which John Wesley usually stayed when he came to the town to preach. This he did fourteen times, the first visit being made in 1747. He wrote in his journal that he had ridden over from Zennor to the little town of Newlyn: 'This was at five in the evening and an immense multitude of people had gathered together, but their voice was as the roaring sea. I began to speak and their voice died away.' When he returned the next year however he describes being met by a stone-throwing rabble when he began preaching: 'They were nevertheless still and quiet as if they felt all that was spoken by the time I had done.' It seems he was thought well of in Newlyn and as an old man of eighty-six he made his last visit in 1789. That year, on the morning of 21 August, he preached in Newlyn and in the evening at a venue in Penzance. The thatched cottage was pulled down around 1883 and so this little piece of Newlyn's history was lost.

Newlyn Old Harbour, 1880s

Fish jousters waiting for the fleet to unload in the old harbour area. One is reminded again by the composition of this photograph of works by the Newlyn School artists. Certainly the group on the left and the painting 'Fish Sale on a Newlyn Beach' have a resonance. The first reference to a quay at Newlyn was in 1435 when one Edmund Lacy made an appeal that was recorded by the Bishop of Exeter 'to all who should contribute toward the repairing of a certain quay or jetty at Newlyn, in the parish of Paul.'

NEWLYN TO LAND'S END

Victorian Street Scene, Newlyn

Surely one of the Newlyn School painters was hovering with sketchbook and colours when this sunbathed study was made in Newlyn. One can see it translated so easily by Stanhope Forbes, or Harold Harvey, in lavish stroke impastos of fresh pigment and high colour.

Newlyn, 29 June 1885

The publication here of the following three views across Newlyn gives me a chance to correct an error of mine in the book I put together in the 1970s. Not long after publication I discovered that the Gibsons walked the foreshore from Penzance to Newlyn on 29 June 1885, the day the foundation stone was laid for the South Pier, taking views across as they went. Nearly all of the exposures they made that day can be identified by the appearance, in the far distance, of the pile structure that had been erected to allow work to begin on the pier. There are quite a number of images in this series of which three are included here.

In the top photograph of fish jousters waiting on the beach, the piles can hardly be made out in the distance. But in the lower two images, looking across from the Tolcarne (middle), and the view from the Old School Slip (lower), the structure is seen quite clearly far left.

Charles Campbell Ross, the local MP, was to lay the foundation stone. The day was it seems well-blessed with good weather and the Gibsons made the most of it, producing a splendid set of prints.

The pier was opened for service in 1886.

Newlyn Fishermen, c.1900

Crews of Newlyn fishing boats in the days of sail.

Newlyn, 1890s

In the 1960s Tony Pawlyn of Newlyn acquired from the then failing Frith company a set of original plates of Newlyn. These two in the book are made from direct contacts. They need little explanation except to say that both date from the 1890s. The net mending is taking place in Newlyn at Vine Cottage, still there today in the lower Newlyn back streets, and the old fisherwoman was a common sight around the town. Alathea Garstin remembered her calling at the family home when she, Alathea, was a little girl. The fisherwoman was given a new petticoat by Alathea's mother each Christmas as a present for supplying them with fish through-out the year, whereupon she would pull up her skirt to display the petticoats she was wearing, a little to Norman Garstin's embarrassment, and to the fun of the rest of the family.

Newlyn Old Harbour, 1890s

This is a classic example of the photographic style of the Francis Frith company. In the latter part of the nineteenth century they put out sets of full-plate and half-plate views of much of Britain and then, when the postcard craze began in the late 1890s, continued to publish these in that format for many years. This scene is on the road that runs through what is known locally as the Newlyn Narrows, continuing as it does to Mousehole. The original title for it was 'The Cliff, Newlyn'.

Early 1900s, Newlyn

This photograph appears to show the old lady going inside for her purse to pay the fish jouster, whilst her dog looks on. This charming cottage has now been greatly altered, and is called 'Quay Cottage', which may be the original name.

Trembath Mill

The fast-running streams of West Cornwall travel relatively short distances from their sources in the hills to the sea. This made it necessary for the water mills, built almost everywhere in suitably watered valleys in the eighteenth and nineteenth centuries, to be constructed for overshot working. Quite a small stream could be made to power a relatively large mill by this method. The overshot wheel has a number of buckets built into its perimeter, moved by the weight of water fed into them and filling them from the top, whereas, the undershot works by the force of the water flowing up to and under it, requiring the heavier weight of a substantial river flow to force the wheel around. These are mainly found in flat, low lying, counties.

The water supply for the overshot mill wheel is diverted off, some distance upstream, into what is called a leat or race, and runs along to a storage pool, there to be controlled as and when required by a sluice, feeding water over and into the wheel buckets. In this way also, a river or stream source, just a few miles long, could be made to work a number of mills, providing power all down its length for a variety of purposes.

Trembath was one of three mills to be found on the short journey from the nearby hills of Newlyn River. At Newlyn town's edge was Tolcarne Mill, then approximately one mile upstream. Trembath was next in line, and about three-quarters of a mile on, just beyond Buryas Bridge, lay Nancothan Mill. Both Tolcarne and Trembath sported two working wheels, the biggest at Trembath being 25 feet in diameter, the largest in the Penwith area. The buildings, as photographed here in the winter, shown without much vegetation to obscure them, offer a visual tribute to the great rural granite workings of this period in Cornwall.

Overlooking Mousehole, c.1870 and 1900

The two views presented here, looking over Mousehole fishing village, allow for some comparisons. The first was taken when the south arm of the harbour was under construction which dates it as 1870. The second was taken around the end of the nineteenth century from Raginnis Hill Road. The south arm of the harbour was officially opened on 14 October 1870.

Newlyn, 1890s

More net mending in Newlyn. This time the Cotton family are engaged at it outside their cottage in Primrose Terrace.

A seaplane port, referred to elsewhere in this book, was later to be established where the far cottages stand, and after that Penlee Quarry was opened on the site. The link road between Newlyn and Mousehole now runs through here.

Mousehole Harbour, c.1910

Mousehole harbour showing nets hung up to dry after 'barking', probably at Mr Tregenza's establishment. The barking process was carried out to preserve the nets by dipping them into a solution called Catechu, extracted from the heartwood (not the bark – despite the name), of certain East Indian trees. The word was shortened to 'cutch' by local fishermen. Barking was another of the many activities associated with the fishing industry that provided work for local craftsmen – in this instance coopers who made the barrels and wooden pans to hold the cutch. See also the photographs on page 34 of men washing the barking pans in Newlyn River and the photograph of hundreds of baskets piled up by the water's edge, evidence of the local cane-workers' skills.

Mousehole, late 1800s

Mousehole harbour in the late-nineteenth century when it was still very busy as a fishing village. This well-known print, much published, was nevertheless not one I felt I could leave out of the collection as it conveys such a good feeling of the place and time.

Mousehole, c.1900

Mousehole harbour as seen towards the end of the nineteenth century. This south-west corner was then known as Fishermen's Square.

Lamorna Valley, late 1800s

Lamorna Valley is today known by tourists for the beauty and lushness of its wooded hillsides, the tree-shaded road winding down through hedgerows to the harbour and postcard-pretty cottages. When this photograph was taken in the latter half of the nineteenth century, and for well into the twentieth century, a rather different scene would have presented itself to the visitor. This was an important quarrying location. Horses and wagons hauled stone away up the dusty road, quarry men (who lived with their families in the cottages seen here), blasted and hammered their way into the hillside, shattering the silence of a summer day. Cove fishermen would also have added to the animation, as they often supplemented life at sea with work in the quarry. Bosava Mill, just a short way upstream from the harbour, would have been busy grinding the local farmers' corn, as would Clapper Mill at the head of the valley road, where Stanhope Forbes stood sketching it for his large painting entitled 'Clapper Mill'.

St Buryan, c.1890

I have a number of photographs in my collection of Cornish churches, but none as attractive as this one of St Buryan Church, near Land's End. Its high tower makes it a conspicuous landmark from miles around. It is quite large inside too, the nave being 58 feet long and the chancel 43 feet. The village has a rich history documented back to early Saxon times, and in myth and legend well before.

47

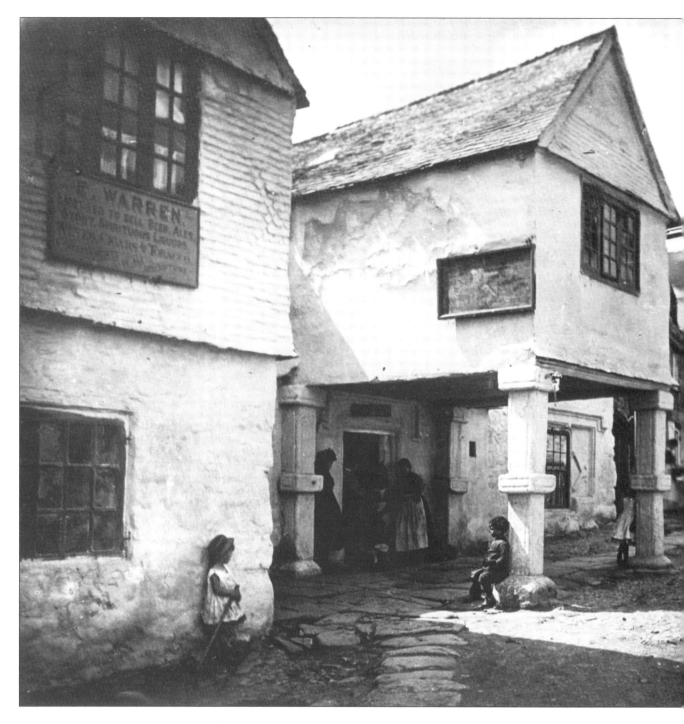

The Keigwin Arms, Mousehole, 1880s

This is one of the only remaining examples of a fifteenth-century Manor House in West Cornwall. That it has survived is fortunate, since the rest of ancient Mousehole was burnt to the ground by an invading Spanish force in the reign of Queen Elizabeth I. On the morning of 23 July 1595 the Spanish came ashore under the command of Don Diego de Brochero, some 200 of them from the four galleys in the bay, lead by Don Carlos de Amesquita. They killed Jenkin Keigwin, whose family house this was, despite the defence he put up against them, and they went on to burn Paul church and attack Newlyn and Penzance. They withdrew to their boats hastily after soldiers arrived from Plymouth and Sir Francis Drake's ships sailed around after them from the Lizard. A detailed contemporary account of this can be read in Richard Carew's *Survey of Cornwall*, 1602.

Penberth Cove, 1871

Two views of Penberth Cove located approximately five miles from Land's End. The cove has fortunately escaped the ravages of thoughtless development, in spite of the fact that even when these photographs were taken, the cove was well advertised in Penzance as 'a picturesque venue for tourists and sightseers'. The landau waiting at the top of the slip has probably carried people out on a sightseeing tour. The settlement was established around the middle of the seventeenth century and the view looking upriver shows the pilchard pressing shed and fishermen's cottages, all still there today. Church Rock is clearly seen on the hill. Today many more trees have added a soft lushness to its former stark appearance.

Telegraph Company Excursions

Two dapper groups of telegraph company employees. The photograph above shows the clerks of The Eastern Telegraph Company posing outside their first station building on 9 November 1871, one year after it was erected. The other, more cavalier looking party seen below, are from the competition. These are the gentlemen of The Western Union staff at Portreath, splendid chaps all of them. Their local headquarters were in Penzance.

I've written in some detail thirty years ago about The Eastern Telegraph Company but I must confess I know little about The Western Union. I'm therefore recommending that readers visit the excellent museum opened at Porthcurno, in the old cable and wireless buildings.

The *Granite State*, Porthcurno Bay

After hitting the Runnel Stone Rocks, the wind jammer *Granite State* was towed into Porthcurno Bay in November 1895, where the captain and crew were taken off by rescuers. Bad weather came in again and eventually she broke up. Her cargo of wheat, originally meant for Swansea, was lost. To the left of the sea line is the Logan Rock headland.

Porthgwarra, 1890

Billy Harvey mending crab pots. This beautifully composed photograph was by J.C. Burrow ARPS, whose work appears throughout this collection. The original print from which I made this copy negative was in the possession of the late George Burrow of Hayle, grandson of J.C. Burrow, though I had seen an example of it and made a negative some years previously from another source.

Aground at Pardennack, 1908

Well and truly high on the rocks at Pardennack, near Land's End. The Lowestoft fishing boat *Girl Annie* went ashore in thick fog on 4 May 1908. All the crew rowed safely ashore, although one of them did break his arm trying to climb the cliff in order to establish where they were. This photograph has a fine visual impact, the result of excellent technical work by the photographer, yet having been an event that, for those actually the subject of the drama, was certainly unwelcome if not a total disaster. I feel one should always be mindful of these things when viewing such scenes, but admittedly there is a fascination in such events.

The *City of Cardiff* Wreck

Three hours were required to restore this photographic image from a faded, murky original. The type of rescue in progress here, using a breeches buoy, is very rarely seen and I've never found a better example, so the effort was well worthwhile.

On 21 February 1912, the *City of Cardiff*, on passage from Le Havre to Cardiff, went ashore on the Land's End side of Nanjizal Bay in thick fog and heavy weather caused by a west-south-west gale. Things weren't helped by the fact that she was in ballast and running high in the water. The crew were rescued but the ship was a total loss. At low water even today her boiler is still visible.

St Michael's Mount, Penzance.

Kelp Gathering, Mount's Bay, early 1900s

This fine view of St Michael's Mount shows an activity that was once very common throughout the whole of Mount's Bay. After a storm, or certain other sea conditions had deposited seaweed in quantity across the beaches, farmers and others would gather it up to put on their fields and vegetable gardens.

Early Motoring

From the beginnings of the motor car it was considered a must, it would seem, to visit Land's End from all parts of the country. The top and middle photographs were taken in 1904 and 1908 respectively. Here, hotelier, Ben Trehare, is seeing off these intrepid early motorists.

All Aboard! Marazion, 1902

If the date of 1902 written on the back of the original print, from which I made a copy negative, is correct, then this local bus venture was ahead of the Great Western Bus Company in running a service between the two towns. The Great Western didn't begin until 30 November 1903. I'd be watching out for those two characters peering from the back window on the return journey in the evening after closing time!

**Marazion Hotel,
c.1905**

A Milnes Daimler bus of the Great Western Railway Company in Marazion main square. The service to Marazion from Penzance began on 31 November 1903. This photograph was probably taken quite soon after, as this was one of the earlier vehicles used by the company.

St Michael's Mount, 1894

This photograph of 1894 was one of a series that A.W. Hughes and J.C. Burrow took that year. It seems the two friends intended publishing together a folio of prints to be titled 'From Cadgewith to Perranporth'. Hughes was a clever technician with a keen sense of composition, as this print shows, and J.C. Burrow had just had published '*Mongst Mines and Miners* in 1893, a magnificent achievement of underground photography. I was shown the collection of photographs the pair had taken by the late George Burrow some twenty years ago. He was a grandson and the unfinished project was in album form, having been handed down to him through the family. We became good friends and I made copy negatives from it. Several other prints appear elsewhere in this book. It was not clear as to why the project was never finished by them.

St Michael's Mount Harbour

In the latter part of the nineteenth century the vessel shown here, the *Henry Harvey*, belonged to Captain Jagoe of Marazion. Built by Harveys of Hayle as a schooner, she was launched in May 1857. Intended as a sailing collier, she nevertheless had an extra large hold to enable the carrying also of machinery and boilers made by Harveys. By the time we see her here she had been altered to a brigantine. During her working life she went deepwater, as well as doing coastal work, and went aground several times. In 1898 she became stuck on Battery Rocks off Penzance, but survived. In 1906 she and her crew tragically disappeared for good while on a voyage to Brittany.

Madron, c.1870

This splendid photograph of the King William IV Inn at Madron was published in my book thirty years ago but I couldn't leave it out this time. Its rustic charm dates from the 1860s to the early 1870s, when John Michell was the landlord. I'm not quite sure what the crop is that is growing out of the roof thatch! Old thatched roofs in Cornwall were prime habitats attracting adders in the summer. Some years ago an elderly acquaintance, living in an old cottage down the Cot Valley, near St Just-in-Penwith, had a crop of grass growing out of his thatch and a sizeable number of snakes to go with it. These could be spotted sunbathing from the path above his home on the approach to the house.

Rural Charms

No photographic collection would be complete, surely, without a glamour section, so this is it. The first of these charming studies is of a Sancreed girl, but only the photographer's name, J.F. McClary of Drift, Penzance, survives on the portrait, taken about the late 1880s. The other portrait is of Dora Chapple of St Levan, taken c.1900 by her husband, Charles Roberts Chapple, an enthusiastic and talented amateur. Posing with the pet dog was obviously all the fashion, I've three other examples amongst my collection.

HMS *Warspite* ashore at Prussia Cove, 23 April 1947

There are quite a large number of photographs to be found relating to the battleship HMS *Warspite* as its demise, after it broke loose from tugs towing it, was much reported at the time. She was being taken to a Clyde shipbreakers when a fierce south-westerly gale and heavy seas ended with her being driven hard on to rocks at Prussia Cove. I've chosen to show this particular one because it's strange to view this huge vessel lurking in an almost sinister way just off Prussia Cove with the small boat and lobster pots as a contrast.

Gulval, early 1870s

This cottage and its outbuildings in Gulval, near Penzance, were already ancient when photographed in the early 1870s. With several animal pens, a small one probably for a pig or hens and a larger one for a donkey or cow, the picture gives a unique glimpse into an even earlier era when rough-hewn granite, cob and thatched dwellings of the same character would have been a general feature of the villages and countryside throughout Cornwall.

Rosebud, **PZ87, 20 October 1937**

This is the Newlyn fishing boat *Rosebud* leaving harbour on 20 October 1937, skippered by Cecil Richards of the town, with a picked crew of fishermen. It is at the start of a 450-mile voyage to London, eventually to sail up the Thames to hand in a petition signed by 1093 Newlyn residents to the government of the day. Their action was in response to the firm intentions by sections of the enlarged Penzance Council to demolish much of Old Newlyn, their cottages, fishing lofts, workshops and all other buildings, and to erect 'more suitable' dwellings in their place. The outcry locally was unanimous and fishermen, craftsmen, shopkeepers, architects, artists and all the old residents contributed to the resistance. The advisory committee they formed made pleas and protests but these were swept aside and the fishing boat petition was decided on to raise national awareness of local feelings of anger and frustration.

National newspaper coverage was good, with photographs of *Rosebud* sailing up the Thames, and the petition well received but that was all. Demolition began and was only halted by the outbreak of Hitler's war in 1939 which put a stop to housing development everywhere in the country.

Newlyn School Artists

The first of these two photographs is of Norman Garstin and Mrs Garstin, and another artist-to-be sitting on her mother's lap, Alathea Garstin. It was Alathea who showed me the Victorian Cornish photographs she had purchased from the Gibson and Preston studios as a girl. That was to be approximately sixty-eight years after this photograph of her with mum and dad was taken in 1894.

Norman Garstin had, just a few years earlier in 1889, donated his now famous painting featuring Penzance promenade, 'The Rain it Raineth Every Day', to Penzance town.

The second photograph, taken some fifty years later, shows Stanhope Alexander Forbes (1857–1947) in his studio. Forbes has come to be called the father of the Newlyn School but Norman Garstin was very much part of the beginnings of the movement in Newlyn as well, and I have a recording by Alathea talking about her father's part in the school, just before she died in 1978. There is a painting of Mrs Garstin, by Norman, wearing the hat you see here.

AVIATION PIONEERS

The Combined British, Atlantic and Mediterranean Fleet, Mount's Bay, July 1910

There's not an aeroplane in sight in this Gibson photograph of the combined British, Atlantic and Mediterranean Fleet but I'm including it here as it shows the scene taken in the year of Claude Grahame-White's first flight over Penzance, on 23 July 1910. A postcard was published at the time commemorating the two events, superimposing Grahame-White's Farman aircraft on to the picture of the fleet. Peter London, in his book on *Aviation in Cornwall,* mentions in detail how the aviator, to prove a point, asked for permission from Admiral May to drop an object on the flagship *Dreadnought*. The national newspapers noted the offensive capability of the aeroplane by stating the frail aircraft would have avoided all efforts to bring a single gun to bear upon it. An amazing forecast of things regarding the eventual importance of military air power.

Grahame-White's First Flight in Cornwall, 23 July 1910

The statement made in the title above refers to the first flight by a heavier-than-air machine propelled by an engine. Jack Humphries of Fowey had, in 1902, designed and successfully flown gliders, which might themselves lay claim to the first flight in the county.

Arrangements for the flight depicted above were hampered all that day by gusting winds and it was not until 6pm that these died down enough for the Farman biplane to be prepared in front of the gathered crowd, who each had paid 2s.6d for the privilege of viewing the spectacle. The field chosen for the take off was named Poniou Meadow, belonging to Poniou Farm, just east of Penzance. It was 8pm when all was finally ajudged satisfactory and the now-restive crowd were rewarded for their patience with a brief three minutes of flight at a height of 200 feet and cheered, so we're told, with great excitement. A second flight was decided upon as dusk was approaching and it was nearly 9pm when Grahame-White took off again heading west for Newlyn. While over Eastern Green, Vaughan Paul, a Penzance professional photographer, literally grabbed this fine dramatic record of the historic event.

Continuing, the aviator passed over Chyandour and Penzance town, amazing people in the streets as he flew on toward the promenade and Newlyn before turning east over the sea. Here, he made several circles over the British Combined Fleet, some 200 ships anchored in Mount's Bay for an informal review by King George V. They in turn blew their whistles and sirens in salute and it was all a great success. The flight had lasted about fifteen minutes and covered nine miles. Huge cheers again greeted his landing.

That same year Grahame-White came second in the *Daily Mail* London–Manchester air race. He gained a time advantage over other competitors by fitting his biplane with car headlamps so that he could take off at night. How engaging and clever of Vaughan Paul to include a portrait of this early aviator inset on to the photograph.

Gustav Hamel's Flight, Penzance, 1913

On 4 September 1913, just over three years after Grahame-White's first flight in West Cornwall, Gustav Hamel surprised the Penzance townspeople as he flew over the Market House. He had been invited to come as the guest of Mr Jeffrey Amherst (later Lord Amherst). His venue for this day was Trengwainton, the Bolitho family home. Hamel took off from the grounds, flying over Penzance, headed for Newlyn, circled around St Michael's Mount and then across country to St Ives on the north-west peninsula, before returning to Trengwainton. Later, in the early evening he flew to Land's End being the first man to do so. He was one of the most prominent pioneer aviators and had made several crossings of the English Channel by the time he came to Cornwall. He was also one of the first men to loop-the-loop. The Gibsons, who took this photograph and a number of others of the event at several locations, had obviously set up beforehand ready to make this historic record of Hamel's Bleriot aircraft poised like a kite just east of the flag on the Market House dome.

Trengwainton, 1913

These other two photographs of Gustav Hamel's visit, taken in the grounds of Trengwainton, give a good view of both his Bleriot monoplane and of the assembled company. The line-up in this picture is as follows, from left to right: Mrs Bolitho, Major Bolitho, Lord Amherst, T. Bedford Bolitho, Gustav Hamel, Lady St Levan, Lord St Levan.

It's quite interesting to note that Gustav Hamel does not appear in this photograph of his Bleriot. The man sitting in the cockpit is Major Bolitho with Mrs Bolitho standing alone beside the aeroplane. The identity of the other persons is unknown.

Henri Salmet, Penzance, April 1914

This shows the two-seater Bleriot owned and piloted by Frenchman, Henri Salmet, within the safety of Penzance Dock. He had the aircraft fitted with a float undercarriage at Falmouth following an earlier landing accident there. Previously he had visited Fowey to give an exhibition flight and then at Falmouth, on St George's Day, he circled over the town, landing on Gyllyngvase beach, only to do what is termed a nose-over in the soft sand, fortunately without any severe damage to himself or his aircraft. He had set off for Penzance from Falmouth on 27 April but due to several setbacks was eventually towed round a choppy Lizard Point into Mount's Bay, beaching first at Penzance and then moving into the floating dock as seen here.

Scilly Isles, 1929

The first flight to the Scilly Isles in a land-based aircraft, not a floatplane, was on 19 August 1929. Lord Sempill (as he later became) piloting a De Havilland DH60G Gypsy Moth biplane; he landed it, as recorded in these photographs, on the golf course near Carn Morvah on the north-west side of the main island, St Mary's. He had flown there from a field on the Lizard.

Pentle Beach, Tresco, 1930

This is the Wright Bellanca WBZ NR237 'Columbia', pulled up above high tide on Pentle Beach on the eastern side of Tresco, Scilly. It's in the evening of 10 October 1930. Flown by Captain Errol Boyd and Lt Harry Connor, their intention was to fly non-stop from Newfoundland to Croydon airport but on approaching this first point of land over the Atlantic, their aircraft developed fuel tank problems and so they landed it on this narrow stretch of sand. It was dragged up above high tide for the night and tied down. The next day they completed their intended journey after repairing the fuel tank, with spare fuel being brought from Mount Batten by a Southampton seaplane of No.204 squadron. The pilots took off from the beach and their arrival in Croydon was greeted by a large crowd.

RNAS Newlyn

In January 1917 The Royal Naval Air Service floatplane base at Newlyn was established by the Admiralty. This was done to increase the network of Cornish stations for both floatplanes and land-based aircraft in the fight against German U-boats during the First World War in the Channel. The two other nearest stations for floatplanes were at Padstow and Tresco on Scilly.

The first of three photographs I have selected here gives a good view of the floatplane port, looking towards the cliff, and of its general make up. In front of the Bessoneaux hangars, as used at Newlyn, on its beaching chassis, is a Short 184 (N2988) floatplane. The cottage nearest the flagpole was the officers' mess, now demolished, the other cottage is still there. Later quarry workings took over this location.

The other two photographs also show floatplanes, one viewed from the interior of the station (with heavy handling marks on the print which I've decided not to retouch). The other aircraft (N2631) is being beached before hauling up.

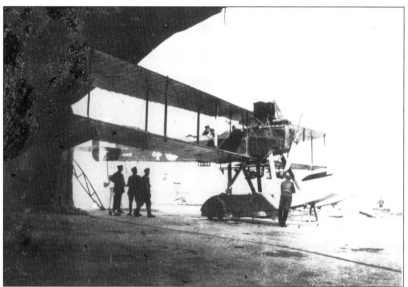

How I came by these rare prints in the early 1970s is a story that demonstrates the good luck one sometimes has when searching for archive images. In this instance I was helping to hang photographs and paintings in the Newlyn Seamen's Mission, when an elderly man appeared clutching a wallet from which he produced for our viewing, six small snapshots. These were taken, he said, with a Vest Pocket Kodak camera owned by his father, who had served at the Newlyn station. They were little contact prints, very worn and well-handled, as the thumbprints enlarged here, along with the image, denote. When I asked if I could make copies of them, he readily agreed but said he was only down for a few hours from upcountry. I

therefore took them up to my studio on Newlyn Hill, copied them, checked the negatives, returning them in less than two hours. He left almost immediately, before I could properly check his name or contact address. Having never seen him again I'm unable to acknowledge the amateur photographer who provided us with this fine historical record. There are very few others in existence, I've only seen two apart from the other six I copied.

Short Calcutta Flying Boat, Porthcurno, 30 May 1928

This Short Calcutta flying boat G-EBVG was photographed by another aircraft that accompanied it, a Supermarine Southampton S1231. It's on a trip to Land's End along the Cornish coast from Plymouth. It is sure to have excited great interest as it passed harbours and villages.

Airship over Sennen, 1930s

This exciting and dramatic photograph was taken from fields overlooking Pedn-men-dhu headland, at Sennen, near Land's End, around 1936–37. It's from a Box camera snapshot negative. Peter London, the aviation authority, has identified it as either the Graf Zeppelin or the Hindenburg. The outline of the then German national insignia for civil aircraft and airships can just be made out on the fins of the phantom-like cigar shape floating through the mist. The people seen assembled (also just visible in the lower fields) would have been treated to the muffled drone of the engines as she made passage over them. How delighted the amateur photographer must have been when he or she, having had their film processed, saw that they had captured the event so forcefully. I encountered some problems whilst enlarging, to achieve a satisfactory print from the original Box camera negative which had much deteriorated. On the envelope containing the negative was written, GAF Zeppelin, Sennen, so Graf Zeppelin is what I'm settling for.

St Eval, Shackletons

We end this section of archive aviation with these photographs of Shackletons flying in formation, near St Eval on the north coast. In 1952, when they were taken, St Eval was the main coastal command station for the area with a total of 24 Mark I and Mark II of these aircraft resident there. I've selected them, as for years after this they continued in search and rescue over the seas around our shores and were held in high esteem by everyone. The original prints from which I made these copies had been consigned to the waste bin in 1954 during restoration and refurbishment of a control room on the airfield. There a young Mr Brian Pannell, a St Eval station fireman doing his RAF National Service, already had a keen sense of collecting historical documents and took charge of them. In the first, the formation is flying towards Bedruthan Steps, clearly seen on the coastline, and St Eval airfield is on the right of the immediate landfall. The second is taken from the airfield itself. The third is taken from another aircraft and shows a Mark I Shackleton over the sea. There is still a Shackleton Club with membership made up of those who flew these aircraft.

HIGH DAYS AND HOLIDAYS

Glamour on St Ives Beach, 1931

This lovely gaggle of girls was captured with a snapshot Box camera in the early 1930s. On the back of the contact print, from which I made this enlargement, was written 'St Ives, Whit Tuesday 1931'. Just that, but the fun in the picture speaks for itself.

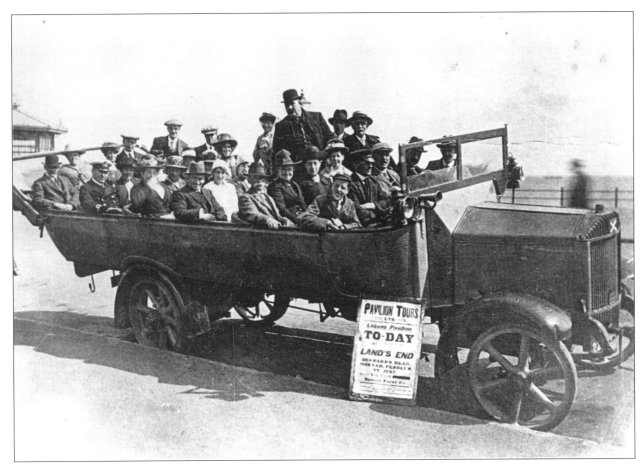

Penzance Promenade, early 1900s

Leaving for Land's End at 2.35pm, as soon as the photographer has done his job. Considering some of the hills they are about to encounter on the tour specified, and the cable and rod brakes part visible, the sea of smiling faces is in contrast to that of the driver. Note how he sits looking resolutely, perhaps even grimly, ahead.

Wesleyan Guild

This fine group photograph of the St Just Wesleyan Guild on one of their summer outings is a great favourite of mine. It was taken by William Thomas of Ballowal Place, St Just, a talented amateur photographer, as much of his work proves. The Guild went one year to Sennen Cove and the next to Porthgwarra Cove, driven there by Archelaus Thomas in his horse-drawn, open Jersey. That's him with the white sun hat on. I've labelled this before as a  Sennen visit but whilst down at Porthgwarra Cove myself the other day, I've decided now that this was more likely to be there. No matter, I've a large framed copy hanging up and it never fails to lighten my day a little when I look at it.

Outside Gulval Old Inn, late 1800s

An outing for the Western Hunt at Gulval. At the time this photograph was taken T.R. Bolitho and W.T. Bolitho were joint masters. Ladies at the time, with proper decorum, rode to hounds side-saddle, as can be seen by the rider, back right-hand side, on the white horse.

Logan Rock, c.1890

This well arranged group photograph was taken by Govier, a professional St Buryan based photographer. It was taken in the 1890s on the clifftop near the Logan Rock in Treen, St Levan Parish. I find one of the most engaging things about it visually, is the texture and pattern of the light and dark dress fashions. The clarity also obtained by the then large-plate negative and slow fine-grain film emulsion, allows for the viewing of the faces portrait by portrait. I would like to think cucumber or egg sandwiches were the next thing on the programme of events, after the excitement of the photograph.

Boat Trip, early 1900s

The *Queen of the Fal* getting up a good head of steam for her day-tripper voyage upriver to Truro or St Mawes. Pendennis Castle can be seen on the Falmouth headland.

Crowlas, c.1900

This charming street scene of about 1900 is at Crowlas, between Penzance and Hayle. Why everybody is dressed up and ready for something has not been recorded, however, and no one seems to be able to shed any light on the proceedings. I feel it could be something to do with a Cornish village feast-day celebration and forthcoming tea party in the chapel (seen in the background). These were often preceded in those days by a march around the village, as was the midsummer celebration day.

Horse Bus Outing

The Penzance Antiquarian Society about to set off on one of their frequent excursions to an antiquity. With two leaders and two wheelers in harness they should make some of the hills without all having to dismount while the horses are led up by the drivers. Certainly, the nearest white horse looks a rather poor thing. These excursion teams were often purchased early in the season, worked hard and finished by the end of it, then to be sent to the knacker's yard.

Camborne, late 1890s

A well-appointed Jersey car of the Camborne Posting Company Ltd, late 1890s.

Out for the Day

Horse and Jersey car, horse and wagonette, horse and haywain, horse and vegetable carts, as here, it didn't seem to matter too much if you had to scale down the cost of the transport as long as it involved being together. Set up high on four wheels and pulled by a willing horse, everybody is dressed in their best bib and tucker; the front groom looks particularly smart. I can't put a name to the occasion or place but the original was in a collection that came from the mid-Cornwall region. I feel it provides an interesting contrast to others shown in this section of the book.

WORK

Shoeing an Ox, near Camborne

This very animated scene leaves us in no doubt about the way to deal with your ox. First get permission to cut down the biggest elm tree you can find and saw it into four stout posts. Anchor these down well. Get further poles and posts, rope strong enough to hold a steamship against the quay, and a good supply of rings and chains. Catch the animal and tell all onlookers to stand clear until he's well and truly tethered. Lastly call the photographer to record the event, as you won't want to do this too often. My friend, Clive Carter, when he saw it felt he'd heard of this taking place at Troon, near Camborne, at a country show, some time around the 1920s.

Knife Grinder, c.1890

This beautifully detailed glimpse of a knife grinder at work is at a location somewhere in West Cornwall. That's what was written on the envelope of the original half-plate negative used by me to make this print. The young girl's dress helps qualify the date of about 1890s.

Madron, early 1900s (opposite)

This photograph is one of two taken at the same time by Richards Bros of Penzance. The blacksmith shown, Jenkins & Son, is at Madron, about two miles from Penzance. I have the half-plate negative original for this one and the print has been made directly from it in my big old enlarger.

Newlyn, c.1890

In the nineteenth and first half of the twentieth centuries, net mending outside cottages and in the streets of fishing villages, was an everyday sight. This is from a quite faded print and shows work in progress on St Peters Hill, Newlyn, in about 1890. Surely there's an artist hovering somewhere, just out of view, waiting to capture this scene on canvas.

St Ives, c.1890

The St Ives workshop of W. Ward, coachbuilder, wheelwright, carriage painter and undertaker. The whole family assembled, late 1880s, early 1890s.

Garage Forecourt, c.1930

This Cornish garage photographed in the first half of the twentieth century just had to be included in the book if only to tantalise the viewer with the petrol price. For those not old enough to remember what we call 'old money', petrol was less than 7p a gallon.

Penzance Harbour, 1930s

A collier unloading in Penzance harbour in the 1930s, demonstrating just how packed and busy it was then (as it still is today). St Mary's Church can just be seen.

PZ196 Sailing Pilchard Driver

A Newlyn fishing crew with their excellent catch, taken around the turn of the nine-teenth century.

Tucking Pilchards, late 1800s

A fine picture of fishermen at sea dealing with a large catch of pilchards. There are men actually in the seine net using baskets to fill and load the catch on to smaller boats. One can see the men clearly on the left-hand side holding the net and the smaller boats alongside. Quite often the procedure was to use these tuck boats, so called because a net from them was used to tuck around smaller numbers of the fish in the seine for easier landing. Percy Craft's painting 'Tucking Pilchards' would have been inspired by just such a scene as this. The photograph was from the late-nineteenth century and several older people I spoke to said it was of a great multitude of these fish that were taken off Porthcurno's Bay, remembered for taking several days to land. This seems reasonable as it would have allowed time for the photographer to hear about it and get out to the scene to record it for posterity.

Pressing Pilchards, c.1930

This shows one of the small pilchard pressing and general processing factories in Newlyn in the late 1920s–early 1930s. The millions of fish caught were salted down and then pressed into special barrels for shipment to the Mediterranean countries, especially Italy, where Cornish pilchards were much in demand. The high contrast in this quite difficult interior for the photographer is due to the use of a limited number of artificial hanging light sources in this windowless loft, plus ribbon flash, still in use up to the 1930s by a number of professional photographers, in certain circumstances.

MINING

Crowns Mine, Botallack, c.1875

This gives a location view of the Crowns group of mines, Botallack, scene of the famous visit by the Prince and Princess of Wales made ten years earlier. On the hill is Wheal Edwards and West Wheal Owls. To get the full effect, if you wish to make a visit to these mines, now ruins, you should go when there is a strong westerly gale active, perhaps just before or after its peak so that you can stand up! Even on a quiet summer's afternoon, sitting with cucumber sandwiches and a flask of tea, viewing the location and considering the men all those years ago going there in the early morning to start work is quite something. Wheal Owls ceased working in 1893, being finished after one of the worst mining disasters recorded in the area. The sea broke in after blasting was ill-judged, opening the workings up to a deluge of water as the sea flooded in. Nineteen men and a boy perished and others barely escaped with their lives. So sad to think of even now, it was the boy's first working day underground.

The Mining Photographs of J.C. Burrow, 1893

The selection of mining photographs that follow (to page 92, top) are from the book *'Mongst Mines and Miners* published in 1893 by J.C. Burrow FGS, ARPS, the Camborne photographer. Thirty years ago I was fortunate to strike up a close friendship with the now late George Burrow of Hayle, grandson of J.C. Burrow. George had a copy of *'Mongst Mines and Miners* in which Burrow's original half-plate contact prints were pasted, illustrating the text. George was only too pleased to let me make copy negatives from which those here are printed.

Burrow, a very clever and talented photographer, was much applauded at the time for this work, which took over a year to accomplish because of the difficulties met. He writes a short piece at the beginning of the book 'How the camera was used'. In it he lists a number of the difficulties presented during the work underground, such as attendants struggling through semi-darkness, falling headlong into a pool of water, with a hydrogen cylinder of 20 cubic feet capacity under one arm and lime light burners in hand.

He writes of magnesium powder in a tin being ruined by a sudden flush of water down from the shaft ceiling, of equipment being dropped down shafts in darkness, and describes the bottom levels where miners worked almost naked because of the heat. At near 100°F the camera lenses steamed up and water vapour damaged his cameras. Burrow tells us that he used a half-plate camera after deciding that a whole plate or

10 x 8in plate camera would present too many problems in confined spaces. He used a Zeiss Anastigmat Series 3 lens made by Ross & Co., which he called 'a perfect gem'. He loaded double dark slides on the surface in order to avoid getting the grease and dirt on them found in the mine. Cadett Lightning plates he found to be very sensitive and unequalled for his purpose. The exposure from the lamps and flash ribbons, on order to his helpers to 'light up', was from two to four seconds; the lens of course being uncapped for this, rather than opened for exposure, by the use of a mechanical shutter.

Very little work had been done regarding underground photography by 1893. As Burrow wrote, 'So many difficulties have presented themselves at the outset that the work has invariably been abandoned after a brief trial'. However Burrow adds, 'Mr H.W. Hughes (mentioned elsewhere in this collection) had obtained some excellent underground results in the coal and limestone districts of South Staffordshire. The difficulties of safety in a coal mine with open powder flash, which was the biggest obstacle, needs no describing here!'

The numbers written on the keyline drawing (below), and the titles used to describe the features seen in the photograph (opposite), used as the frontispiece of *'Mongst Mines and Miners,* are those given by Burrow in his 1893 publication. The drawing represents the group of mines on the north side of Carn Brea Hill in the tract of land between Camborne and Redruth in 1893. Carn Brea monument can be seen on the far hill, top right, with the Castle House a little below.

1. The Old Stamping engine at Dolcoath. 2. The New Californian Stamps. 3. An engine here pumps water from a shaft. 4. Dolcoath Eastern Shaft. 5. The Dolcoath Valley Smithy, where Richard Trevithick is said to have performed much of his work. 6. Cook's Kitchen Mine Office. 7. Cook's Kitchen Mine pumping and winding engines. 8. Cook's Kitchen Mine Stampings and Dressing floors. 9. New Cook's Kitchen Mine. 10. Tincroft new pumping engine. 11. The North part of Tincroft Mine. 12. Carn Brea Mine South part. 13. Carn Brea Mine North part. 14. East Pool Mine in the distance. 15. Carn Brea Castle. 16. Carn Brea Monument.

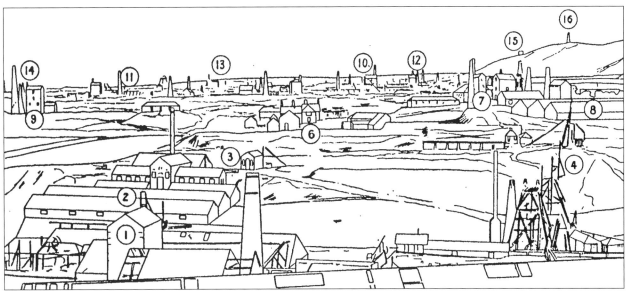

The Man Engine at Dolcoath Mine, 1893

This, we are told, was taken at the 234 fathom level. The photograph shows clearly how the miners travelled up and down to the different working levels. Several miners are standing on the man-engine step which will be moving up and down, driven by the steam-powered engine on the surface. When he reaches a sollar, as the fixed platforms are called, the miner steps on to it and waits for the next step to reach him before stepping on to that. In this way he proceeds up or down the shaft as required. As can be seen, one man waits on the platform whilst the other travels up or down on the moving man-engine step.

The Balance Box at Dolcoath Mine, 1893

Photographed at 236 fathoms, the only way Burrow was able to get this dramatic photograph was to climb over the box and fix the camera to look down on top of it.

East Pool Mine, 1893

The tram-road in East Pool at the 180 fathom level. The lode had already been worked well away and we see an almost cathedral-like space above the tram-road. Ladders are used to reach the levels below and above.

Cook's Kitchen Mine

Timbering above the 406 level at Cook's Kitchen Mine. It was to supply the mines with timber supports and beams that large areas of Cornish woodland were cut down in the peak years of the industry.

The 406 Level, Engine Shaft, Cook's Kitchen Mine, 1893

This photograph shows how, by 1893, quite a lot of mechanisation was in use below ground as well as on the surface. An air-winch is being used to draw the raw ore and rock drill workings from the bottom of the shaft. The pumps and iron pipe conveying compressed air to the rock drill are formidable structures above the skip road.

Croust Time, Cook's Kitchen Mine, 1893

The miners, having performed the first part of the day's labour, are taking a break for something to eat. Croust is the name the Cornish give to this. Quite often blasting of the next workings was done before croust so that the smoke and dust would have time to settle before resuming work.

Carn Galver Engine House

This magnificent photograph is of the Cornish engine houses and beam engine near to Carn Galver, on the parish boundaries of Morvah and Zennor. Called Carn Galver Mine, it was also referred to by the 1857 name of the mining sett it stood on, St Just and Zennor United. The company holding this name also had the properties of Ballowall, Nanpean and Bosorne Setts, near to Cape Cornwall, in the early 1880s when this picture was made. The ruins can still be viewed today on the side of the St Just-in-Penwith to St Ives coast road, standing proud against the skyline, having weathered Atlantic storms for well over a century since it ceased working.

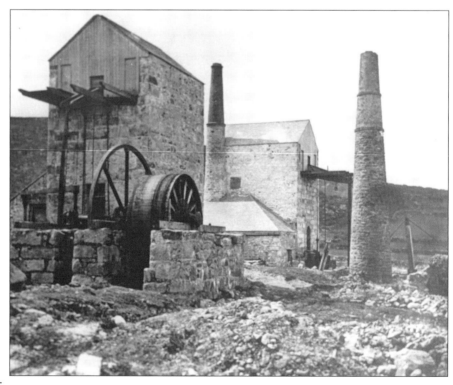

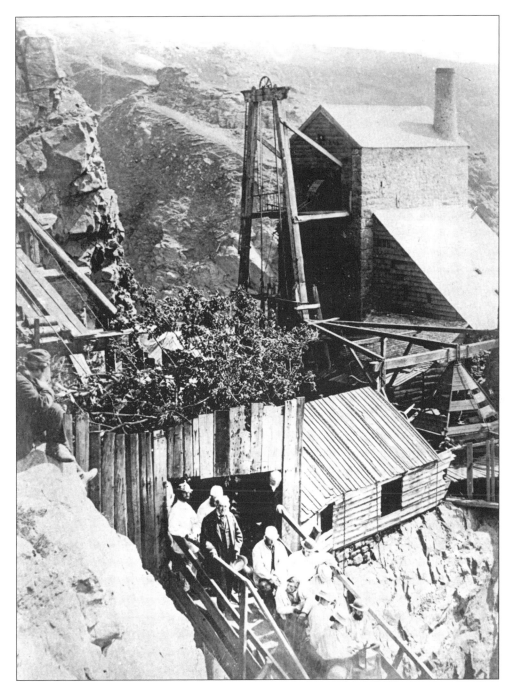

The Prince and Princess of Wales visit Crowns Mine, Botallack, 1865

This is now a well-published photograph of a Royal visit to West Penwith in the nineteenth century but one which I've selected again for its impact and sheer brilliance of Robert Preston's photography. On Monday, 24 July 1865, the Prince of Wales and Princess Alexandra, under the protective guidance of the mine captain, Henry Boyns, visited the Botallack group of mines near St Just and descended the Boscawen diagonal shaft of the Crowns Mine. The Princess and her lady-in-waiting wore special protective capes made for them by a Heamoor woman.

Although the original from which I made the copy negative had begun to fade badly, especially at the bottom, you can (with the little enhancement I have given this print) discern the Princess sitting in the specially fitted-out gig, behind the lantern, as they begin their descent. This diagonal shaft was over a mile long and went well out under the sea. It is reported that afterwards she felt giddy and somewhat shaken and was driven quite quickly in the Royal carriage to St Michael's Mount.

Looking at the location and at the general structural conditions, and considering the journey under the sea, one can't help fully sympathising with the young Princess's dilemma after making it safely back to the top, even with the able Captain Henry Boyns in charge. The mine went bust in 1895 and was closed down never to open again.

Cook's Kitchen, 1893

The man engine at Cook's Kitchen Mine which went down 215 fathoms below the surface. A gig that would hold six men was put in the engine shaft in 1888 to carry miners to the deepest part of the mine.

St Just United Mine, c.1890

This shows the group of mine workings just south-west of Cape Cornwall, one of the properties of the St Just United Company. This is on the Ballowall and Nanpean Mining Sett as drawn up in 1857, the company also owning Bosorne and Ballowall adjoining this, along with Carn Galver on the Morvah–Zennor Parish boundary. Opened in the mid 1870s at the height of a boom in demand for tin, it was soon turning out a ton of tin a day. However, as anyone knows who has read even a small amount about the late-nineteenth-century tin mining in Cornwall, the sudden slump in prices, due to cheaper sources being found abroad in a number of locations, easier and cheaper to mine, meant a collapse in the price of home-processed tin ore. This mine closed, like a number of others in the area, in 1889. The exodus to the Americas and elsewhere, by Cornish miners became a flood. By the turn of the nineteenth century shipping companies in St Just and other Cornish mining areas were offering voyages at just £10 a head. The headland in the background is Cape Cornwall, the only promontory in the British Isles named a cape!

St Ives Consols

The immediate past of St Ives is now associated in most minds with fishing and with artists, and today of course very much with tourism. However, when this photograph was taken, around the 1870s, mining was going on both on the very perimeter of the town and all around in the nearby countryside. This shows the dressing floor of St Ives Consols Mine.

Levant Mine, Pendeen, 1894

This is another of the photographs taken by H.W. Hughes on his walking photographic tour around West Cornwall in 1894, along with J.C. Burrow. It shows the old Levant Mine at Pendeen. Some years ago a young Scott Tutthill of Penzance, a good friend, wrote this poem which was published once just before he died. He gave me a copy and, in memory of him, I would like to include it with Hughes' photograph here as I feel it fits the occasion so well. Ding Dong Mine, referred to at the beginning of the poem, was in its heyday one of the richest workings in Cornwall.

Song for Past Cornish Miners

Ding Dong, Levant and old Wheal Jessie,
Standing like bad broken teeth
in the jaw-bone of the Cornish land.

Are these the giants of the legends?

Singing in the man engine,
Light song in darkness and seeping damp.
Songs of joy and youth in the open bath house.

'Old Hundred' chanting in the mist
and fog of the March dawn.
'All people that on earth do dwell
Sing to the Lord with cheerful voice.'
Stump, stump of the engine's heart beating.

Songs of glory and of joy,
Rushing up, up on the waves of heat,
From the rumbling intestines
of Earth's great stomach.

Scott Tutthill

CLAY MINING

A Devon man, William Cookworthy of Plymouth, was motivated to find clay in his native country which could reach the high kiln temperatures required to give the smooth, dense body required for porcelain manufacture. Up to the end of the eighteenth century no one had been able to crack the secret of making this fine pottery held by the Chinese for over a thousand years. 'Kaolin', or as they said, 'kaoling', named after the Chinese discoverer, was the main body agent used and, in 1755, Cookworthy, more by accident than design, discovered deposits of the white clay on Tregonning Hill, near Mount's Bay.

Soon, however, he came across much larger deposits at locations near St Austell; north of the town at Hensbarrow and west of it in the parish of St Stephen in Brannel. It was quite soon referred to as china clay for the obvious reasons, and the whole area of St Austell became known as the china clay region, or simply 'Clay Country'. A.K. Hamilton-Jenkin, writing in 1934, called it the 'white country' and goes on to say how everything in the locality was white: dumps, streams, pools, the stacks of white clay, the men themselves, as they walked home from work with powdered chalk-like faces. Such conditions are well illustrated here in the group photographs I have selected.

In 1810, at the beginning of the clay mining industry, there are records of only seven small family-worked pits. These early workings were never very deep and were abandoned for new excavations as soon as the ingress of water became difficult. The clay-bearing granite was crushed and mixed with water to form a slurry. A series of washing and settling processes separated the white decomposed feldspar from the other impurities, not least of which was quartz sand. It was this sand that was piled up in the countryside around the pit. Quite small in the early days, workings gave way eventually to pits a mile round, hundreds of feet deep, with pyramid-like hills, as high above ground as the pits below. The slurry having settled in suitable troughs and pans was cut into blocks and cleaned by women, 'Bal Maidens'. It was then transported by horse and wagon to the Pentewan and Charlestown harbours, and later to Par Docks. With the expansion of this most important Cornish industry in the twentieth century it all eventually became, as one would expect, highly mechanised, and amalgamations of businesses into much larger groups followed.

A Clay Dry, c.1910

One of the sheds known as drys, used in the late-nineteenth and first half of the twentieth centuries, to dry the china clay slurry after processing it from the rough-mined decomposed granite. The chimney at the end drew heat from a furnace under the liquid clay, driving off the excess water.

Bal Maidens

Before the days of mechanisation the china clay mined and processed was eventually made up into blocks to finally dry. This was usually the work of 'Bal Maidens', seen here.

China Clay Workers, early 1900s

Both group photographs demonstrate A.K. Hamilton-Jenkins' description, in 1934, of the white world around St Austell. The height of the summit of the waste tip which the four men are standing on can be felt by reference to details in the surrounding countryside. The engine-house chimney on the left of the picture for instance, its top is still well below the level the men are standing on.

West Hill, St Austell

Here the blocks of clay have been transported from the nearby pits to West Hill, St Austell. They were then loaded into trucks and taken to Pentewan, or Charlestown harbour (and in later years to Par Docks), for shipment to all parts of the world.

Coasters, Par Harbour

Sailing ships waiting to take on china clay loads at Par.

STEREO IMAGES

Stereographic View Cards

Since these cards were very popular with people for entertainment in the nineteenth century, and continued so well into the first half of the twentieth century, I thought it both fun and necessary to include just a few examples here. In the Victorian and Edwardian era special viewers were used, such as the Holmes type hand viewer, to achieve the three-dimensional effect. The two lenses of the stereo camera and the two lenses of the viewer received pictures of a subject, just as we do through our eyes, our bifocal vision combining the two images to give the sense of depth and space. You can, however, achieve a three-dimensional effect from the photographs without a viewer if you can get the knack of 'free viewing'. To do this, hold the double pictures just a few inches from your eyes, then draw the page slowly away from you. Keep staring at the two images, without allowing your eyes to converge. As the page reaches a certain distance away from you, about twelve inches to eighteen inches, the three-dimensional effect should occur. If you wear glasses for close reading put these on. You may need to make a number of attempts at first. It's true to say that some people, due to eyesight defects, will never be able to achieve this effect. I hope, in any case, you find something of interest in this selection of views. The first dates from the 1860s, but stereo pictures were being attempted within a short time of the birth of photography and Daguerreotype stereo photographs exist still, from the end of 1840. With the introduction of the wet collodion process in 1851 stereo cameras also began to appear to meet the technical demands of that process.

The Logan Rock, Treen Headland, 1860s

This large boulder could be rocked ('logged') when pushed, from the south-west side, as you can see the man demonstrating for the photographer. In 1824 Lieutenant Goldsmith RN with a group of his crew, who I should think were in a rowdy state of mind, famously dislodged it. Public outcry resulted in them replacing it, at quite a personal cost, but the rocking was never the same. Several good lithographic and aquatint illustrations of the replacement were made to sell to later visitors. Those that turn up at auctions now are keenly sought after by print collectors.

Newlyn Fisherwomen, late 1800s

A group of women fish jousters pose for the photographer on the north quay of Newlyn harbour. This was fully lengthened and opened as complete on 3 July 1894. Considered too narrow, however, by a number of users and critics, it was widened in 1895. These women went from door to door around Newlyn, Penzance and surrounding villages with fish purchased direct from the fishing boats on landing.

The Keigwin Arms, Mousehole

This stereograph was made about twenty years later than the earlier one shown on page 48. Refreshment rooms and furnished apartments are advertised in the signboard by R. Richards, the owner at the time.

Newlyn Harbour, South Pier, early 1900s

The south pier was the first of the two long quays built to improve Newlyn harbour. The foundation stone was laid after work commenced on 29 June 1885, by Charles Campbell Ross MP and finished towards the end of 1886.

Newlyn, c.1909

Looking west towards the old harbour. The *Elizabeth and Blanche* lifeboat, having recently been moved from Penzance, can be seen under wraps up on her launching carriage.

Mill Ruins, Nanjizal

This print shows how a stereograph, when properly viewed in 3D, comes to life from what appears to be a fairly ordinary 2D image. It's in a West Cornwall valley and shows the old mill ruins at Nanjizal, on the cliffpath from Porthgwarra to Land's End.

Looking Towards Pardennack near Land's End

Penzance, St John's Hall, c.1900

Penzance, c.1900

Looking down Chapel Street, Penzance, towards St Mary's Church in the very early 1900s. The house directly behind the tree was the home of Maria Branwell. As a young woman she was to become Maria Bronte on marriage, and was mother to Charlotte, Anne, Emily and Branwell of literary fame.

Looking up Market Jew Street, Penzance

The statue celebrating the life of Humphry Davy, the Penzance-born scientist and inventor, can be seen clearly in front of the Market House. The monument was erected in 1872.

St Michael's Mount from Marazion

SCILLY AND SAINT JUST

St Mary's, Scilly, 1871

This view over Scilly from Buzza Hill was taken by Gibson in the spring of 1871. It shows clearly the *David Auterson,* barque-rigged and 264 tons, the last ship built at John Edwards' yard on Porth Cressa Bank. She was launched in late spring of that year. She was not the last ship built on Scilly, this honour goes to *The Gleaner*, 178 tons, launched in May 1878. Looking across one can just see the Star Castle and, left, the Duchy State House.

Group Portrait Study, Scilly Isles, about 1871

Augustus Smith, born in Hertfordshire in 1804, educated at Harrow, graduated at Oxford Christ Church College in 1826, is seen here, towards the end of his life, surrounded by Scillonians, for whom he had worked and devoted most of his interest for over thirty-seven years up to 1871. On 20 November 1834 he entered into an agreement with the Duchy of Cornwall for the lease of the Scilly Isles for a term of ninety years. With it came the responsibilities of both estate management and the reforms necessary if any new proprietor was to get to grips with the inadequate administration adversely affecting the islanders' economic and general living conditions left by the previous leaseholders. On 3 November 1831, after various legal wrangles, the property reverted to the Duchy from the Godolphin family to whom it had been bound since 1571.

When Augustus Smith took it over he was well aware of the many problems, having researched the island life well before entering into the agreement. He was a man of tireless energy and advanced theories on social reform, which he was anxious to put into action. This he immediately set about doing with a persistence and well-considered policy to restore prosperity and bring about a new order. St Mary's inhabitants had endured poverty and hardship which was also a constant part of life for the inhabitants of the small off-islands. Augustus Smith organised the islanders as a whole. He had of course almost a free hand to proceed as he felt fit, providing that he could carry the people with him, and this he did, eventually winning great respect from them for the improvements he brought about.

In this carefully arranged photograph by John Gibson, we see Smith is smiling, obviously pleased with his life's work. The men around him are a cross-section of the island farmers, fishermen, pilots, shipwrights craftsmen and estate workers. Census records for 1851 number almost a hundred different crafts, callings and trades pursued by the relatively small island community, not counting those various divisions of crafts-men wholly engaged in specialist areas of shipbuilding.

St Mary's, Isles of Scilly, c.1870

The main street in Hugh Town, St Mary's, Scilly Isles, in the early 1870s.

St Mary's, Isles of Scilly, 1871

Looking across St Mary's towards Buzza Hill with its old windmill seen clearly on the top. The *David Auterson*, in John Edwards' boatyard and Porth Cressa beach are now on the right. On the extreme left there can just be made out another boat under construction.

St Mary's, 1870s

A view across from the Garrison. There is a lot of detail in this photograph but it is not so sharp as the previous views over the island. The animals, or is it animal, in the field centre has moved during the exposure, giving a clue to it being of a possible two–four second duration, which has also caused the blurring in the vegetation.

Tresco, early 1870s

This view, taken on Tresco, shows the old quay. Across the bay, near to the farm and chimneys, was the site for the seaplane port when they were stationed there later in the First World War, as mentioned in the aviation section of this collection.

Tresco

View over Tresco before the construction of the new Grimsby quay, showing the abbey roofs.

Scilly, late 1800s

In 1867 a Mr Trevellick Moyle, of St Mary's, packed a cardboard box with a few bunches of daffodils, which grew everywhere on the islands like weeds, and sent it to Covent Garden market. He did this, it is said, at the suggestion of Augustus Smith. Whether this is so or not, he eventually received half-a-crown for his trouble and was encouraged to proceed further. He joined with two other men to plant out more bulbs in fresh ground and the encouraging returns from the venture convinced them that they were on to a good thing. Then others joined in and the Scillys' flower farming industry had started. By 1896 600 tons of flowers were sent to the major city markets on the mainland. All hands are given to bunching up here, except the dog sunbathing.

Gathering Kelp, Scilly Isles

A donkey, patient and obedient, waits while his owner gathers kelp. This will be spread on the field or garden before ploughing, or piled up in heaps and covered in sand to rot down first. It made a very good manure providing it was not over-used.

Sennen Cove, late 1800s

This is Mrs Grace Nicholas at the entrance to her general stores. Questioned by J. Harris Stone, we are told, gathering material for a book, *England's Riviera*, she informed him that she had already been married twice but was now looking for her third husband in order that he could provide the money for a set of teeth she needed! We look into the picture over the rowing boat used by Trinity House and its lighthouse keeper when relieving the Longships. The hand-winch was used for pulling it up the slip.

Sennen Cove, 1870s

Sennen Cove is situated almost at the very top of the south-west Cornish peninsula, approximately one mile from Land's End on the north coast. This is the earliest view over the cove which I have been able to find. In John Corin's book *Sennen Cove and its Lifeboat* he refers to it as a fishing station, pointing out that there is no semblance of a natural fishing harbour or cove but rather just an inlet in the cliffs. The village is certainly open to all the weather the Atlantic throws up at it, and the combination of a westerly gale at its height and high tide attracts visitors in large numbers to view the spectacle from the safety of their cars. The onshore rollers break over the harbour and slipway, diffusing up the hillside and over the cottages.

   Looking into this view there are specific details which help date it approximately. It's certainly before 1886 as there is no sign of the wooden loft added to the capstan house that year. This would be located clearly behind the long group of buildings where much of the fish was processed. There is however a man-capstan seen above the slipway that leads down to the old narrow entrance and breakwater. In the centre on the shoreline is a two-storey building with tall double doors. That is the first lifeboat house. Various other features, or rather in some cases lack of them, gradually steer one to date the photograph around the 1870s. The original from which I made the copy was an albumen print and, as is often the case, well faded. I have enhanced the contrast when making the print but otherwise, as throughout this book, no tampering with detail and content has taken place.

Sennen Cove, c.1900

The negative for this was from an early small folding camera and had the thickness and general feel of roll film stock as used at the turn of that century. The stone slipway leads up to the capstan house with its wooden loft, added in 1886. Inside is a large capstan. Rigged down sailing crabbers stand by the wharf.

The Success Inn, Sennen Cove, c.1900

Seen here at the end of the nineteenth century, the 1896 lifeboat house can just be made out in the mist at the right-hand side. An inn was established here in 1691 and the Old Success, as it's now called, is today one of the best-known inns in Cornwall.

Sennen Cove, late 1800s

Unloading pilchards in Sennen Cove. A seine boat and loader boats are being discharged. The man stand-ing up in the boat in suit, coat and hat is probably a buyer. Some of the fish would be taken direct to the pressing house in baskets.

Sennen Cove, c.1890

Here seine fishing boats and loaders wait to discharge their catch at the bottom of the old 1886 timber slip. Most cove fishing in Cornwall was done either in family or individually-owned boats but seining could not be done in this way due to the expense involved in providing the seine boat, usually over 30 feet in length and a seine net some 300 fathoms in length, by seven fathoms deep, plus attendant tuck boats and loaders. It was therefore worked by the formation of a company with funds to back the outlay involved. These companies were loosely affiliated and quite often changed names, were sold or split up. The Sennen Fishing Company could actually afford a steam seine boat and in this picture she can be made out by her chimney well out in Whitsand Bay in the upper left of the scene. Other companies had names such as 'Success', 'Fishermen's Friend', 'The Old Company', 'The Speedy' and 'The Penwith'. The crews worked on a share basis, after the owners or promoters had taken their share. I'm told it could get very complicated at times!

Sennen Cove Lifeboat, *Newbons*

A legacy from the estate of Mr R.A. Newbon of Islington provided for a new 40-foot self-righter lifeboat and this arrived on station, as seen here, on 1 May 1922. As a motor lifeboat she replaced four sailing and pulling lifeboats. The arrival of a first motor-powered boat was greatly welcomed but the RNLI continued to maintain on board a set of spars, sails and oars in case the single 45hp petrol engine failed. She went on to give nearly thirty years' service, saving lives at sea off this treacherous coastline.

Sennen Cove, c.1890

Another picture of pilchards being unloaded in Sennen Cove, towards the end of the nineteenth century. This is a great favourite of mine. The animation of the event and the unknown photographer's arrangement of composition content are so clever and full of interest. I was introduced to an elderly couple, some thirty years ago, who lived in the cove and, having expressed interest

in photographs, was entertained by them all evening with tea and cake and books of their family snaps and views. However, these weren't quite what I was looking for and after thanking them for a pleasant time, I was just leaving when I caught site of this photograph in its original decorated Victorian frame and backing. They were kind enough to loan it to me for a day or so. A very exciting discovery. I have a sepia-toned copy hanging on the wall of my room at home.

Sennen Covers, 1870s

An interestingly arranged group photograph made by Robert Preston. The albumen print original dates it around the 1870s. The photograph is taken close to the lifeboat house.

St Just-in-Penwith, 1930s

Market Square. I understand from an enthusiast that the vehicle seen parked in front of the hotel is a rare glimpse of an even rarer Morgan three-wheeler car. A more common machine, but much loved, is the little Austin Seven parked in front of the paper shop.

Market Square, St Just

The Great Western Railway had intended continuing a branch line to St Just but it never came about. However, on 16 May 1904 they did commence a bus service to the town from Penzance. This is a Straker Squire bus outside the Commercial Hotel in Market Square. Sam Woolcock stands on the right of the photograph by the back wheel. He was the first of the Woolcocks to take over the Commercial in 1902 and it has continued in the family ever since. Paul Woolcock runs it now.

Horse Bus at Penzance

The Royal Mail horse bus rounds the Alverton bend as it enters Penzance. The horse omnibus, operated by Archelaus Thomas of St Just, continued in service carrying the Royal Mail from that area of Penzance up to the end of 1920. This was sixteen years after motor transport buses had run a service to the town, as he still retained the Post Office contract. It has been claimed that a Mr Brendon of Bude operated the last horse-drawn vehicle in the county to carry the Royal Mail, up until 1919, but actually Archelaus Thomas of St Just was the last, having continued for a year longer.

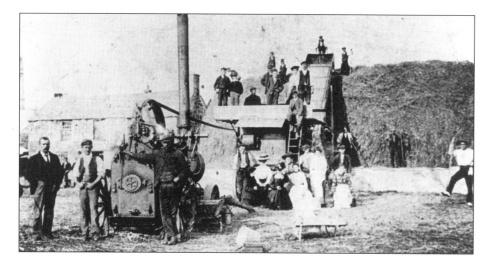

Gews Farm, St Just.

Threshing, West Cornwall.

Threshing mid Cornwall.

Harvest Home

The threshing scene. Who can resist viewing such images, especially if they have ever had the experience themselves, as a child, of being at the threshing party tea; the smell of the straw and tractor exhaust, even possibly steam oil, if you're old enough. I recall the fun, the falling off the unmade stack, and eating dusty sandwiches with fond affection. The first of these three scenes shows threshing at Gews Farm, St Just, about 1900. Mr Prissy Jelbert owned the stationary steam engine. The other two came from West Cornwall and mid Cornwall; I have no further definite details of them but does it matter? I think all ages can view these pictures of animation, light, work and fun and be moved by them.

THE SOUTH COAST

Inner Harbour, Porthleven, c.1900

Pilchard drivers and crabbers form the bulk of the small craft in this once very busy fishing village. There could also be one or two sailing smacks engaged in oyster dredging in the Fal area, though most of the sailing smacks engaged on this would have been kept nearer the Helford and Fal fishing grounds.

Introduction to W.M. Harrison prints

The photographs on pages 123 to 128, page 132 (top) and on pages 134 and 135 were produced as commercial tourist photographs by the Falmouth-based photographer W.M. Harrison. The copies which I made were from full-plate originals in what was a studio stock album for showing to customers. Harrison's specialisation was in topographical landscape and studio portraiture. The portraits were competent and stylish but it is his landscape works that particularly arouse my interest, for they show an original approach and use of technique that are both sensitive and so very much in sympathy with the chosen localities. These, starting from the south-west range from Porthleven and Helston, continue along and through the Helford Creek area around the Lizard Point, taking in the Fal River and Falmouth to Truro. The lushness of the deep wooded valleys and mysterious creeks, quiet meadows and open sweeping beaches is so well presented, as you will see for yourself. The massive cliffs of the immediate Lizard shoreline, however, seem not to have influenced his choice of content for picture making so much and there were only a few examples in the album.

Whether he knew or was influenced by a now highly recognised contemporary, I have not discovered, but his work bears similarities to that of Henry Peach Robinson's rural scenes. 'Wayside Gossip' comes immediately to mind when I look at Harrison's 'Cleaning vegetables for Helston Market'; the composition, though different in arrangement, has a content which can be compared easily and is so alike in technique and finish. Others here, one feels, Peach Robinson could easily have been author of; see the quiet, beautiful 'Port Navas, Helford' plate. The still water and figures are frozen by his camera in a landscape from which you can hear only the ripples lapping the shoreline. Others such as 'The River Fal' and plate 'Helford Creek' ooze with atmosphere. W.M. Harrison also covered, in a similar way, the north coast from Portreath to the Perranporth area. These are included elsewhere in this work.

Harbour Mouth, Porthleven, c.1900

Porthleven looking over the harbour mouth area to the south-east and Loe Bar.

Cleaning Vegetables for Helston Market

The photographer's title is that used above. This scene is located approximately where the present park and Coronation boating lake have been constructed, just outside the approach to Helston town.

Coinage Hall Street, Helston, 1870s

By the chapel wall, note how Harrison, the photographer, has scratched out a figure moving whilst the exposure was taken. This gives a clue to the date. He was still using slow wet plates; it is after all a sunny afternoon so the light was good. As mentioned earlier regarding the photograph of Penzance on page 20, the faster dry plates were not generally available until 1878.

Port Navas, Helford

281. Helford Cre

Helford Creek

King Harry Ferry, River Fal

This famous ferry crossing is named after a chapel on the eastern side, the Chapel of our Lady and King Henry VI. On the western shore is Trelissick.

The River Fal

Kynance Village

Thomas's Inn, Free House, is clearly seen just right of centre in this excellent composition. The original in this case was rather faded and so, lacking crisp tonal values, I've tried to redress this in the printing.

Mullion Cove, c.1900

Mullion is located just off the A3083 road that links Helston with the Lizard. Continuing through the village leads down to the cove. This is how it looked around 1900. Mullion Cliffs, far left, leads on to Gull Rock and then, middle to right, to Mullion Island.

Kynance, 1890s

This print of the quite remarkable cliff and shoreline formation of Kynance Cove was made from an original quarter-plate direct. The work of an amateur of the time, there's nothing amateurish in the way he has composed and presented it. Two deep valleys lead to the craggy serpentine cliffs and stack. High cliffs border the cove.

Shipwreck on the Lizard

The Lizard peninsula, and particularly the immediate vicinity of the Lizard headland, has been the grave-yard of countless ships over the centuries. I could have presented on these pages a score of images to testify to this statement but I've selected these four as they illustrate, as well as any, the dark, forbidding grasp the cliffs and undersea rocks have had on vessels. Like a spider's web, once in, the chances of escape were nearly always out of the question.

Adolf Vinnen

The first of the four photographs shows the *Adolf Vinnen* ashore in Housel Bay, just below the Lizard Point. Powered by ex U-boat engines, she was on her maiden voyage, out from Brunsbottel, sailing in ballast having come through the Kiel Canal, on destination for Barry, South Wales. All the crew were rescued by lifeboat and breeches buoy. The skipper sailed afterwards in other ships and, it's said, he always lowered his colours in respect and thanks to his rescuers when passing the Lizard Point.

The *Gunvor,* 29 May 1913

This superb vessel foundered just north of the Lizard between the Point and Coverack. On passage from Chile to Falmouth, to have come all that way and be within so short a distance of one's destination when disaster strikes is a hard sentence, and sobering thought regarding life's sudden twists of fate.

The *Hansy*, 13 November 1911

Originally a British-owned ship, here she was owned by a Norwegian company carrying timber from Sundfvall in Sweden to Melbourne. All the crew, once again, were saved by the lifeboat and breeches buoy.

The *Suffolk*, September 1886

Thick fog and a fault in navigation brought about the demise of this steam sailing ship in September 1886. She was carrying cattle and, although all the crew were saved, none of the poor animals survived. For weeks afterwards dead steers were being washed up around the coast, presenting a sad and gruesome sight.

The Lizard Lifeboat

Cadgwith by E.W. Hughes, 1894

This photograph follows on easily from the last photograph, Kynance being on the south-west side of the Lizard and Cadgwith just round the Lizard Point on the south-east. It's an example also of how the Victorians would drop in a sky using another negative if the one that they were able to capture wasn't very interesting. Plates were only blue sensitive and a very bright sky with light clouds would produce too high a contrast for the emulsion of the day to handle, so giving a complete white cloudless sky. They redressed things by a little cheating, or is it? Just think what photographers are doing now with digital technology! This was one of the photographs Hughes took in his photographic tour with J.C. Burrow.

Coverack

Looking across the cove to the old harbour.

St Keverne, c.1910

Several miles north-east of the last photograph of Coverack Cove. The village of St Keverne provided this friendly exterior shot of the Three Tuns Inn. A favourite exterior of mine.

Falmouth from Trefusis

St Clements Church, near Truro

Gyllyngvase Beach, March 1903

The collier *Renwick* aground on the beach after a storm. She was eventually refloated.

Trefusis, near Falmouth

Truro, early 1900s

I have to admit to my collection of Truro City prints being sparse, and of those, the only one I feel merits a showing here is this. A well-published view with the cathedral, designed by John Longhborough Pearson, rising majestically above the old houses, Mallett & Co. warehouse, which is still there, and the river.

St Mawes

I have several prints of St Mawes but have chosen this one with its superbly kitted-out yachting master (well, I feel fairly certain that's what he is), striding along the harbourside.

St Mawes remains the fashionable and, on high days, exciting face of yachting in this area of Cornwall, just as it was in the early 1900s.

Mevagissey Quay, 1913

Clara Martyn of St Austell gave me this excellent photograph of Mevagissey taken in 1913. There are two girls in the picture, the taller one being Elsie Solomon. I know this because the little girl in white told me so when she gave me the original print in 1997. She's Clara Martyn, born in 1908. She remembered clearly the photograph being taken, but she couldn't remember the photographer's name. Mr Farrows had a coal store nearby. That's him smiling, standing with the horse and cart. There was also a fish store on the right.

Mevagissey Harbour, c.1900

The *Volountaire*, Fowey, 1915

St Keyne, c.1900

St Keyne is a few miles from Liskeard where this beautifully organised photograph of N.S. Lander & Son's roller flour mill was taken. I couldn't resist purchasing the original in its fine Victorian frame when I saw it in an antique shop and I'm pleased to think of it being published for others to see here.

ST IVES AND AROUND

Hayle, 1906

This sharp, detailed view over Hayle town was made by J.C. Burrow ARPS in 1906. The excellence of his technique allows for close scrutiny, with a magnifying glass, of the detail in this once very busy harbour complex from St Elwyn Church in the far left to the foundry area and other works on the right. The industrial heritage of Hayle has largely been eroded by neglect and lack of proper consideration from the right quarters, (wherever that might be). However, Cyril Noall's writings of the town are of great interest. Its great part in the industrial revolution of the West Country is well covered by him. As a port for passengers, many people left the town for the Americas, sailing first to Bristol and then on from there. Harvey's of Hayle, owners of the foundry and other important industrial plants in the town, was a name known throughout the world. Ship building was developed from the 1830s on, particularly for the coastal trade, although some deep-water ships were constructed. The largest vessel to be built and launched in Hayle was the 4000-ton SS *Ramleh* in 1891. I drove through the harbour wasteland of Hayle recently and find it difficult to comprehend how this once vital artery in the county's economic life could have descended to the present state. It has so much still that commends it and one can only hope that quite soon this will be realised and properly developed.

Haymaking, c.1941

From a set of six negatives I've selected these two of the haymaking war effort, taking place in fields near St Erth village in about 1941. I'm presenting it particularly for the nostalgic benefit of former Land Girls everywhere, like these, who lived in specially erected wooden hut barracks in a field at the back of St Erth Parish Church. No doubt their lives were filled with lots of laughs and larking about, along with the more serious business that helped to win the war. Later the girls were moved out from their shed-like billets which were taken over to house Italian prisoners of war, but conditions were deemed too tough an environment for the men to live in! They were therefore rebuilt with brick for greater comfort and warmth. Well, that's a story put forward to me by one old local whom I met in the pub.

West End Hayle, early 1900s

Hayle Foundry Square, early 1900s

The drivers, conductors, bosses and general administration staff of the Cornwall Motor Transport Company had obviously not reckoned on it raining when it had been arranged in advance for the photographer to come. This looks like an advertising photograph. They are certainly not 'ready for the off', as I've seen it titled in one publication. Off where?

The Cornwall Motor Transport Company was started by Commander Hare. This ex-naval officer it seems did much to introduce bus services to many parts of the county in the first half of the century. These were in due course absorbed into the National Bus Company and later Western National. All three vehicles are four-ton Bristols but I'm not dating this print precisely as I have no firm knowledge of it. I've already seen three different dates given in other publications.

Experienced vehicle enthusiasts may find the registration numbers of the vehicles of use. On my large print I can just make out for the right-hand vehicle, below the company initials, CMT the letters AF, a Cornish registration, then 8753. On the bus left of the hotel, again below the company initials AF 8752. Buses were kept in a yard behind the White Hart Hotel in the earlier years of the 1900s as the town was for a while, I'm told, one of the terminus points for the company's operating services. The photograph was by William Terrill but I can find no other references to his work locally. However, he's done a splendid job here under difficult conditions.

Hayle, c.1900

Unloading coal in the busy harbour.

Penpole Terrace, Hayle, 1890s

Hayle, January 1895

This photograph, taken by J.C. Burrow, shows the great disaster of the Glasgow collier SS *Escuriel*, on 25 January 1895. The Hayle lifeboat *E.F. Harrison* arrived on the scene after being pulled over the cliff road from Hayle. She had immediately attempted a launch but her carriage had sunk into the soft sand. Frantic efforts by coastguards and assistants, and spectators of the drama, eventually managed to get her launched. One man from the collier had managed to swim ashore but it was the second man whom the lifeboat stopped to pick up which put paid to the rescue attempt. Whilst he was being dragged on board, seas hit the lifeboat in such a way that she was washed back and beached and all further attempts to launch her were useless. Some further rescues were made by people running into the seas from the beach as survivors were tossed ashore by the surf but eventually 11 men perished.

Hayle lifeboat station was manned for fifty-four years from 1866 to 1920 using three different boats. In 40 service launches, 95 lives were saved, and in June 1886 Coxswain Edwin Trevaskis was awarded the RNLI Silver Medal for long and valiant service.

Treveglos Farm, Zennor, c.1895

My family and I lived in this farmhouse for a while in the 1960s but the wonderfully thatched roof had gone by then, as have most of the thatched roofs that once were to be found everywhere in the county.

Tremedda Farm, 1920

The Italian barn at Tremedda Farm, Zennor, and goats to go with it. The barn is still there but the goats have gone. The barn was designed by a relation of Mr and Mrs Griggs who farmed Tremedda for many years.

St Ives, 1890s

Artists at work on the harbour beach in front of the Sloop Inn.

Alfred Wallis, Artist

A gathering of the Salvation Army. The man with the bowler hat, front right, is the artist Alfred Wallis. Once a deep-sea sailor, then the town's rag and bone merchant, and finally, primitive painter, whose works have since found acclaim and admirers far and wide. Both Alfred and his wife were faithful followers of the Salvation Army and I've stood on a summer's evening by the harbour beach, as they must have done on many occasions, listening to the band play. The women of the army would be there in best bonnets, shaking tasselled tambourines defiantly over their heads to the strains of 'Bringing in the Sheaves'. One thinks also, seeing Wallis looking out here, of him working on his dreamlike paintings of fishing luggers and tall ships sailing up the sides of a cardboard panel, out over the fishermen's cottages, through the ink blue seas to Godrevy Lighthouse and beyond.

St Ives Harbour Beach Area, c.1880

The quite amazing way the town's appearance was developed by buildings being built on buildings, others tucked in between, added to, squeezed between, you name it, they did it, is well demonstrated here. Unfortunately planners and developers were to arrive on the scene, but not for some fifty years or so from the date of this photograph.

St Ives, 1890s

Children pose for one of the Frith Company photographers in the harbour beach area of St Ives. There was a quality about the early black and white postcards that seems not to have been equalled in today's productions, except in a few rare cases.

The Digey, St Ives, 1880s

The living area is above the fish cellar where pilchards were dried and salted and pressed. Both cottages have three storeys and the similarity in construction is common to a lot of the other houses in the town. The woman sitting at the top of the steps is, one feels, just waiting for an artist to arrive with brush and canvas.

Back Road West, St Ives, 1880s

A less romantic portrait of the dwellings that crowd the narrow streets of St Ives away from the harbour. More of the poverty of those times is perhaps hinted at in this photograph.

St Ives Shipwreck, 1908

This fine Gibson photograph is a record of a quite remarkable coincidence that began with a sea drama on 7 January 1908 at St Ives. Quite late in the evening of that day the 163-ton schooner *Lizzie R. Wilce* had been driven into St Ives bay by heavy seas, high north-westerly winds and, finally, a failure of sail control. At around 9pm she was forced ashore on to Porthminster beach near the pierhead. She had been on passage from Swansea and was two days out from there, carrying anthracite to St Malo. The St Ives lifeboat was launched and crew and captain were safely rescued. One can imagine the lifeboat men feeling, when all was secured at around midnight, that they had had enough action for one day. This, however, was not to be the end, for approximately four hours later distress rockets sounded off in the bay and this time the 190-ton schooner *Mary Barrow* was the victim. She was also from Swansea, also carrying coal and had left port just a few hours after the *Lizzie Wilce*, and soon she was ashore within a short distance of the other vessel. This is the sight that presented itself to amazed spectators the next day as both ships lay well beached in the Porthminster sands. The *Mary Barrow* was refloated and continued in service as an ocean-going ship. The *Lizzie Wilce* was towed to Falmouth after being sold to salvors.

Pals for Ever

St Ives photographs of the nineteenth century seem full of donkeys posing. This one I've titled 'Pals for Ever', to bring a tear to the eye!

Fire!

Just visible on the print itself was written, 'Market Strand Fire, St Ives'.

St Ives, c.1900

Before donkey rides became popular with tourists, these little animals were essential to the fishing trade in carting goods to and from the beach.

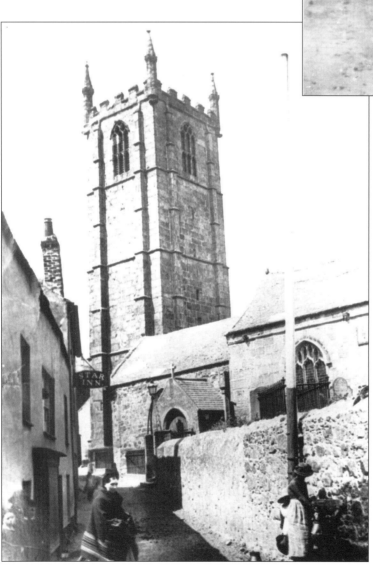

St Ives, c.1870

This photograph of St Ives church dates from the 1870s. The church was completed in 1496. The sign for the old Star Inn can be seen and a woman on the right is filling pitchers with water from one of the town's public water pumps.

NORTH CORNWALL AND INLAND

Camborne, 1903

Tramcar No. 1 posing along with its driver Mr W. Hampton on Centenary Loop at Camborne. The date 1903 was written on the back of my print. Though it makes for a most interesting picture, I can't find out why they are all standing still on this occasion, the policeman, you will note, to attention. If 1903 is indeed the date of this photograph then it's nothing to do with the formal opening of the service between Camborne and Redruth which took place on 7 November 1902. The tramline was soon very successful and a survey carried out found that over one million people had used the trams in less than a year after the service had begun.

Redruth, Fore Street, late 1800s

And once again everyone stood still for the photographer, well, almost everyone!

The Great Blizzard, 1891

The weather on the morning of 9 March 1891 was bright and cold and life in the villages and towns of the county was proceeding at its usual Monday pace. By the evening of the same day the worst blizzard in recorded history had already brought the whole of Cornwall and Devon to a complete standstill. Both on land and off the coast at sea the devastation was building up to a frightening scale. Heavy snow drifting in the high winds was, by nightfall, reaching to cottage upper windows. Intense cold was freezing everything outside, and inside people were finding great difficulty keeping warm, shuttered against the storm. A Mrs Travail, one hundred years old when I met her at her birthday party in 1985, remembered it clearly. She remarked that, 'Our family lived in a good warm house but on this occasion it was so cold we couldn't stop the inkwells freezing up, and all my father's sheep died as we were unable to get them in due to the suddenness of it all.' The newspapers of the time, relying still on line illustrations to support articles, could only offer imaginative suggestions of how things looked, whilst photographers were certainly not able to operate outside in the weather conditions until some let-up occurred. This photograph of the *Dutchman* express train from Paddington to Penzance, with her locomotive *Leopold*, derailed near Stray Park, Camborne, was, I feel sure, a hard-won lone exposure made on 10 March during a brief lull in the storm. Passengers had to huddle in the coaches overnight on 9 March until a rescue was organised the following morning. Many are the stories surrounding the drama of that week. A friend's recording of his elderly grandfather's memoirs mentions the existence of a chocolate salesman on the train who gave his samples to the assembled company!

Stithians Village

Evidently the place to be for school treats around the turn of the nineteenth century, if the baker's van is anything to go by.

Chacewater, Fore Street, early 1900s

This village, situated between Redruth and Truro on the old link road, has retained in its main street much of the character we see here almost a hundred years ago. Its name raises great nostalgia among railway enthusiasts for the part it played in the history of the Redruth & Chacewater Railway. The official ceremonial opening took place on 30 January 1826 when three wagons, carrying the directors and other interested parties, ran under gravity to the new wharf at Narabo. Horses then drew the carriages back to the terminus near Redruth. It was not until 1 December 1854 that steam locomotives operated the service to all the mines and mineral outlets en route.

Smelter

This is *Smelter* one of the first two locomotives to be put into service on the Redruth & Chacewater railway on 1 December 1854. The other locomotive was named *Miner*. These locomotives ended twenty-eight years of exclusively using horse-power, though horses continued to be used for some work after steam came on the scene.

Gwennap Pit

Gwennap Pit in the 1880s and very much as it still is today. John Wesley's influence throughout Cornwall on the religious thinking and lives of people during his lifetime was immense. Gwennap village and subsequently the pit, became a base for much of his work and preaching visits within the county. He began using this man-made hollow having found that it offered some shelter when talking to large crowds. It soon proved also to have natural acoustics that further enhanced the preacher's delivery.

Known to Methodists throughout the world, it has offered a venue for the delivery of services from many famous preachers. On Whit Monday each year since the death of Wesley an annual service is held in remembrance and celebration of his life and work.

Donkey Power

All I know about this splendid portrait of a man and his donkey is that it was taken on a hill above the north Cornish coast. It came with some other plates and prints from the St Agnes to Newquay locality, so I'm slipping it in here before the Portreath and St Agnes areas.

Portreath

The first two views here were taken approximately twenty years apart. The first, by an unidentified photographer, was dated 1905 on the negative, the other is by W.M. Harrison, c.1885. It is interesting to note how much softer the character of the landscape is conveyed in his photography.

Portreath, c.1885

Another Harrison print of Portreath, this time looking out over the harbour to the south-west. Colliers would be unloading here all the time in those days, along with delivering other goods associated with the mining industry.

Portreath, c.1900

This is John Williams and his son Albert waiting on the harbourside with their donkey cart.

Portreath, c.1900

This extraordinary photograph of the *Feedon*, a collier leaving Portreath, has literally been grabbed from the teeth of the wind and sea. Its almost abstract pattern quality has been forced out of the event by the urgency of the whole situation that both the vessel and the photographer have had to deal with.

Trevaunance Cove, St Agnes, 1894

This is another in the series taken by J.C. Burrow and E.W. Hughes for their coastal project. They had titled it 'North from St Agnes'.

Newquay, c.1870

A view across the bay at Newquay. Note the bathing huts on the beach.

Perranporth, c.1900

'Perranporth seen from what was the convalescence home', was how Harrison titled this photograph, taken at the end of the nineteenth century.

Padstow, late 1890s

One can almost feel the sunlight and sense the smell of tar, rope, steam and salt sea in this delightful study. I am unable to give a photographer's name. I found this print backing up another photograph under the frame, full of dust and mildew. For those who don't know Padstow, this is the home of the splendid pagan festival in which the hobbyhorse weaves and wanders through the town on May Day each year.

Bude Canal, 1880s

Harry Thorn and a brother, Samuel, were both active photographers in the area by 1871, and prints of this date bear the imprints of either H. or S. Thorn. Later, a sister joined the business and it is she, Sarah Thorn, who continued the business until well into the twentieth century after Samuel's death in 1898. Sarah died at Bude on 4 June 1932, aged ninety.

Bude,1891

The main street as it looked in the week of the great blizzard that began on 9 March 1891. It was obviously taken when the photographers, Thorns, were able to get out with a camera, once the ferocity of the snow storm had subsided.

Wreck of the *Giles Lang*, 1896

This animated scene on 8 November 1896 is charged with drama as the St Ives schooner, *Giles Lang*, having sprung a leak off Bude, was forced ashore and thrown about in heavy surf. The crew were all saved by breeches buoy. The photographers were the Thorn family of Bude and it could have been taken by Samuel or Sarah, a sister, who by this time had joined the business and continued it after Samuel's death in 1898.

Mr Osborne, Postman at Newmill

I'm stretching the rule I've set by including this photograph since it was taken in the early 1960s, around twenty years after the cut off date for the rest of the collection. It's a favourite snapshot of mine. Mr Osborne, seen here, and his two sisters, ran the Post Office and little stores at Newmill, on the Penzance to Zennor road. Their lives reflected life in earlier times and the Post Office was a perfect time-capsule. The shop entrance door had an unforgettable hanging bell that was superbly amplified by the acoustics of the wooden shop fittings. Further atmosphere was added to the interior scene by the original 1930s wall adverts for products such as OXO and Gold Flake cigarettes, memorable among others. Finally, the bright as a new pin appearance of both sisters and their old world approach to receiving your custom completed the cheery experience of stopping off there to buy a stamp or half a dozen fresh eggs and, yes, there was the smell of paraffin from an oil lamp since only part of the premises had electricity installed and this didn't include the shop area.

Mr Osborne was the last postman in Cornwall to do a large part of his delivery on horseback as far as I can establish. Much of it took him up into the hills and moorland around the famous Ding Dong mining area. Having made that statement for publication I'll no doubt have a letter through my door post-haste tomorrow from someone correcting me and pointing out that there is a postman this very day doing his rounds on horseback in the deep valleys of Helford or up in the higher reaches of Bodmin Moor!